Y0-BDI-712

THE GREAT SOUTH WOODS

II

...more to the story

by Peter V. O'Shea, Jr.

Graphics North

Jay, New York USA

Graphics North
PO Box 218
Jay, New York 12941

© 2005 by Peter V. O'Shea, Jr.

All rights reserved.

Printed in the United States of America

No part of the contents of this book may be
reproduced by any means or used without the written pemission of the author.

Library of Congress Control Number: 2005931787

ISBN 0-9643452-7-7

Book and Cover Design by: Nadine McLaughlin

Cover Photography by: Carl Heilman II

This book is gratefully dedicated
to two intrepid centenarians,

CLARENCE PETTY AND PAUL JAMIESON,

whose efforts in support of
the Adirondack landscape
have long proved
an inspiration to me.

PREFACE

Book I of *The Great South Woods* was published in 2000, and by 2004 the book was sold out; it is now out of print. Due to time constraints before publication, a number of topics that I had meant to include had to be excluded from the first book. Among these were the subject of exotic species in the Adirondack Park, as well as a calendar of nature detailing the progression of the wild in the Great South Woods. I have now tried to adequately address these issues.

In addition, this second book details many of my personal encounters with wildlife over the years, as well as describing my personal philosophy regarding wilderness and wildlife.

Since the publication of the first book, there have also been a number of significant developments in the natural sphere in the Great South Woods. This is particularly evident in the matter of the "Creatures of the Shadow," and I have tried to update these recent occurrences in this second book.

The appellation "great south woods" was the term residents of the St. Lawrence Valley used to refer to the uncharted, sprawling woods to the south of them. This was the area they hunted, fished, and lumbered, an area where the shackles of civilization were not as binding on them as they were in the mill towns and agricultural lands in the valley in which they resided. Generally today, the Great South Woods covers the area within the Blue Line in St. Lawrence County as well as adjacent areas in Franklin and Hamilton Counties.

The writing of this second book on the Great South Woods has been an unalloyed labor of love, like the first one. If the sharing of some of the wonders of this unique area instills in others the penchant to preserve and protect these wild lands that I feel, then my efforts will have been well-expended.

CONTENTS

The Great South Woods II

...more to the story

A night camera catches some strange, yet very like-minded, bedfellows: a porcupine, a turkey vulture, a fox, and a coyote.

Photos by Sue Collins

I
CREATURES OF THE SHADOWS

INTRODUCTION

In my first book, *The Great South Woods,* I found that the chapter on the "Creatures of the Shadow" elicited by far the most comment. The presence or absence of certain furtive, enigmatic carnivores in the Adirondacks is apparently of great interest to a wide variety of people. I was contacted repeatedly by a broad spectrum of folks from diverse areas of the North Country who purported to see these mystery species at one time or another. Others who did not allege to have made a sighting themselves nonetheless knew of friends or relatives who had. There were still others who had a fascination with the topic and wanted to learn as much as possible about it.

In the decade or so that has passed since the writing of the first book, there have been some significant developments concerning the presence or non-presence of these spectacular predators in the Adirondack Park. The Wildlife Conservation Society has advanced the "landscape-species" concept, a theory that considers wide-ranging carnivore species in a broad, expansive, total-landscape context. Under this definition, these predators are considered to range far and wide in their life cycles, uniting diverse habitats and geographic entities. Their need for open, protected space becomes paramount.

The "ghost-species" concept was also tentatively put forth in referring to these far-ranging, furtive species.

The value of protected wildlife corridors, and the crucial role they could play in the preservation and re-establishment of carnivore species, has also been advanced recently. These corridors have been much discussed of late. A lot of this discussion has revolved around the "A-to-A," the corridor linkage between the Adirondack Park in New York and the Algonquin Provincial Park in Canada. Two recent events tend to show that this wildlife corridor already exists in fact, not just in theory. In one of these incidents, a Canada lynx released near Newcomb was shot and killed by a hunter a mere ten miles from the border of Algonquin Park. The other incident was even more definitive. A cow moose named Alice, after residing blissfully in the environs of Newcomb, began inexplicably to wander and eventually crossed the St. Lawrence River into Canada. There she met her demise, smack dab in the middle of Algonquin Park, where her remains were discovered, thanks to the electronic radio collar placed on her by researchers at the State University of New York's College of Environmental Science and Forestry. More convincing proof could not be found, attesting to the existence of a functional wildlife corridor.

Another wildlife corridor traverses the lands of the New York Power Authority, although that state entity considers the corridor to be used only on a local scale. This contention is, in my estimation, refuted by the numbers of moose and lynx that are regularly found on the islands and mainland portions of the Power Authority's domains.

Reports of cougars and wolves, although less frequent in occurrence, are reported sporadically here also. These lands, in addition to the lands of the Laurentian Shield, considered part of the main A-to-A corridor, will also have to be protected. To that end, a private land trust, the St. Lawrence Valley Land Trust, is in the process of being created]. Hopefully, its effects, and that of the larger statewide land trusts, will bear fruit in an open-space valley landscape capable of retaining sufficient integrity to provide for the safe and unhindered passage of these "ghost species" between the Adirondacks and the wilds of Canada.

Following is an update on the creatures that were discussed in the first book. What is readily apparent to me from my unofficial monitoring of these "Adirondack ghosts" is that the rate of sightings and other encounters has accelerated significantly in the past decade.

COUGAR

Reports of this mysterious and significant Adirondack life form have taken an even more dramatic upsurge recently. These reports are being received from all areas of the Adirondack Park and are even emanating from a considerable distance outside the Blue Line.

This situation is most concisely reflected in the recently published

Photo by Uta Wister

Contented cougar at rest.

Adirondack Atlas, by Jerry Jenkins, a project of the Wildlife Conservation Society. The Atlas has meticulously catalogued every report considered to be credible after applying a set of uniform criteria to each report. What has transpired from this detailed analysis is truly a demographic work of art. The map of sightings shows all reports from the 1960s clearly grouped in the Central Adirondacks. After the Sixties, the reports progressively radiate outward until, by the 1980s, it is evident that the entire Adirondack Park is represented. During the following decade, that of the 1990s, this logical progression continues; and cougar reports are shown as transcending the boundaries of the Adirondack Park to the north, west, and even the south.

Another new development in the continuing saga of the Adirondack cougar was the establishment of the Eastern Cougar Network, which set up a website to track what they considered confirmed sightings all over the eastern United States. A strict standard of criteria for confirmation was promulgated; and in adherence to this, a search network was instituted for the entire region east of the Mississippi River. Remarkably, three of these confirmed sightings came from biologists working for the New York State Department of Environmental Conservation, including Ken Kogut, who is currently the senior wildlife manager for DEC Region 5, headquartered in Ray Brook. Any reasonable person would have to assume that these three professional wildlife scientists knew enough about Adirondack animals to know what they were seeing. The wildlife bureaucrats in Albany, however, have resisted this assumption for a variety of possible reasons to be discussed in a later paragraph.

The *Adirondack Explorer*, an environmentalist newspaper published in Saranac Lake, did a series of articles in 2001 that focused on the question of the cougar's presence in the Adirondacks. As part of that series, I was contacted and asked to participate in an op-ed debate as to whether or not cougars were, in fact, actually present in the Adirondacks.

At first, I declined to participate, since I have a natural aversion to taking part in anything that could even remotely resemble a "dog-and-pony show." When I was informed by *Explorer* Editor Phil Brown that the other participant was to be Al Hicks, mammal specialist at the DEC Endangered Species Unit, I changed my mind and accepted the offer with alacrity.

During the debate, Mr. Hicks conceded that he was, indeed, personally aware of two cougars that had been killed recently in and near the Adirondacks; but he steadfastly maintained the official response of the DEC to these occurrences. This official "line" was that all such incidents concerned cougars that had initially been in captivity but that had somehow escaped. I found this position somewhat perplexing, as I was familiar with the circumstances surrounding the demise of one of the cougars, a 16-week-old kitten shot by a hunter in the southern Adirondacks. After the kitten had been shot, the DEC publicly proclaimed that it had escaped from captivity, even claiming that they were fairly certain of the source from whence it had escaped. Conservation Officer Larry Johnson, the lead officer in the investigation, later told me, however, that there was no evidence the kitten had ever been in captivity. He further stated that if his superiors in Albany knew for a fact from whence the cougar originated, they were certainly keeping it a secret from him. Suffice it to say that I made my countering points to Al Hicks in the dialogue; and it would also be fair to say, "the twain never did meet."

I have often wondered what could account for officialdom's stock response to reports of the presence of cougars and other large predators in the wilds of the Adirondacks and elsewhere. Invariably, the reply to the reports either denies their accuracy or claims that animals actually sighted have escaped or been released from captivity. This patented reply is at utter variance with the increasing number of reports — and even the occasional carcass — that keep turning up as the years progress.

My strong belief is that the main impetus for this obstinacy is the Federal Endangered Species designation of the "Eastern cougar." Wildlife agencies feel, and perhaps rightly so, that acknowledgment of cougar and other large predator sightings in the Adirondack Park would put them in the middle of an acrimonious battle between those wishing to protect the cougars and those wishing to eliminate them, because of the financial implication of the Federal Endangered Species Act.

All this becomes somewhat ironic when one considers the results of the recent genetic testing of North American cougars done by Dr. Melanie Culver, formerly of the National Cancer Institute. These results clearly indicate that all cougars on this continent belong to one single, wide-ranging subspecies. The natural interpretation of this extensive survey is that no such creature as an "Eastern cougar" actually exists; hence, it cannot be considered an endangered species.

My feeling is that the cougars now present in the Adirondack Park and elsewhere in New York State should be accorded the same level of protection as is now extended to the moose. The moose is currently considered a game species with no open season. Persons who kill one illegally face fines, possible imprisonment, and loss of a hunting license. This is usually enough to discourage a hunter from shooting a second moose. Most important, however, is that none of the draconian economic implications associated with a federal endangered-species designation are now present; and this almost invariably leads to far greater public acceptance of the species in question. I feel this is the way to proceed in the Adirondack Park and have stated as much several times in public forums and at private wildlife conferences, since a Federal Endangered Species designation could curtail all hunting and logging in the area of impact.

An interesting anecdote that highlights the frustration often felt in trying to validate the existence of these big cats locally is the case of two videos taken by reputable individuals purporting to show cougars in the wild. One was taken in October 2003, the other in May 2004. Both were sent to the DEC's Watertown office for analysis. The one shot in 2004, which had Jefferson County as the locale, was shown on WWNY-TV, Watertown. I did not see the video, since I was in New York City for medical treatment at the time it was broadcast; but many observers I know watched the video and clearly felt that a cougar was depicted. Among those observers were the customers at the Hillside Diner in Oswegatchie, who regaled me with their belief in the video's accuracy. Despite this, the DEC's official response to the video, which was printed in the *Watertown Times*, was that "they were unable to ascertain the identity of the animal in question, but that if it was a cougar it was an escapee and was only passing through." This was also essentially their response to the previous video, shot in Lewis County the year before. This answer covered all the negative bases and rendered hopeless any option of pursuing the subject.

Caution is advised, though, as hoaxes do occur, and indeed appear to be an intrinsic part of the human genome. One such hoax was a photo allegedly taken in the Adirondacks with a camera activated by a motion sensor. This photo was widely circulated, and indeed I first saw it on the wall of my barber's shop in Potsdam. The picture showed a deer running from a cougar. The only problem was that the deer in question was clearly a mule deer, as defined by his black tail, indicating the film was taken in the western United States. The propensity for mindless mischief that some people evince is quite amazing!

When an issue is clouded in such ambiguity and denial, it only seems natural that a whole slew of fanciful assertions will arise concerning the subject. One that I find particularly worrisome has surfaced rather recently. This rumor, which seems to be taking a tenuous life of its own, is that the presence of these creatures of the shadows in the Adirondack Park is owed entirely to the clandestine activities of certain pro-environment groups. This theory first tentatively surfaced in the writings of Dennis April in his regular outdoor column for a Plattsburgh newspaper. Dennis has long had an interest in the subject of cougars and wolves and frequently writes concerning them in his column. I know Dennis, and in fact wrote a chapter in a book he edited on fishing in northern New York, so perhaps some day I'll contact him to see if he possesses any concrete knowledge regarding the matter.

Personally, I do not think this scenario is credible. I have many contacts park-wide and feel that I certainly would have heard if some group or individual had carried out such an illicit act. In addition, ruminations as to the existence of these last carnivores in the Adirondacks have had a life going back at least two human generations. The act would have been unnecessary, as well as illegal.

However, claiming without any proof that "greens" are releasing extirpated species into the Adirondack Park is equally irresponsible. It not only puts the animals that are here at greater risk, it also increases the tension level among diverse factions in the Adirondack Park. Claims that have the potential to do this should only be uttered with due caution.

The regal, furtive feline has always been the embodiment of grace and elusiveness in the Adirondacks, as well as elsewhere. It has also become a symbol as well as a buzzword in the Adirondacks. Ignoring all this, the enigmatic "American lion" continues to go on plying his trade in the Adirondack forest, usually far from the prying eyes of man.

Wolverine

Mention of wolverine presence in the Adirondack Park was made only peripherally in my first book. This was the incident related to me close to 40 years ago by members of the "over-the-hill gang" concerning their encounter with this large mustelid on the banks of the Oswegatchie River.

Despite the fact that I was aware of what could be considered quite credible information, I nonetheless shied away from listing and discussing the wolverine as one of the creatures of the shadow. One of these reported sightings was from long-time friend and expert woodsman, Gaylord Kerr, while the other was from a St. Laurence County DEC forest ranger who prefers to remain anonymous. The ranger was so concerned about not being connected to such a sighting that he informed me that if I told his superiors, he would say that all he had seen was a 40-pound fisher.

At that time, I hesitated to include these quite-plausible reports, primarily due to the lengthy interval between documented wolverine sightings, and also because of the notion prevailing then that wolverines needed the existence of absolutely untrammeled wilderness, entirely bereft of any human presence, to prosper. I also have to admit that my reluctance here was perhaps influenced by fear of ridicule, and perhaps an additional fear of diminishing the validity of the vastly more abundant and concrete reports of cougars and wolves that had long prevailed in the Great South Woods.

As a result, I even ignored my personal experience of coming upon an anomalous pair of tracks one snowy mid-January day. The paired, five-toed tracks, vaguely fisher-like, wove in and across each other's paths as they proceeded through a mature, mixed forest in the woods west of Cranberry Lake. On snowshoes, I followed the tracks for perhaps half a mile until the increasing snow velocity made it pointless to continue any further. Whenever the tracks went across and over one of the many large logs lying on ground, they revealed where the bellies of the animals had distinctly rubbed on the snow, suggesting a chunky porcupine rather than a mustelid. In one place, the creature had dug down through six feet of snow to feed on a deer carcass. I have seen a fisher dig down through three feet of snow on two occasions, but never deeper than that. The clincher came, however, when the pair of tracks dug in still another place through six feet of snow to feed on the roots and stalks of wood fern. In my several decades of fisher tracking in the snow, I had never witnessed this activity or anything like it.

So it was that I blithely ignored all the signs, albeit with some trepidation, until finally a day of reckoning dawned in the form of my own personal sighting of nothing less than a live, flesh-and-blood wolverine! It occurred in the following way: I was walking along an unplowed road adjacent to the Harper's Falls tract of the Forest Preserve when I heard a loud splashing in a wooded red maple-hemlock swamp to my left. All of a sudden, emerging from the swamp at a gallop, came that "chunky" critter (of the tracks), looking for all the world like a cross between a bear cub and a fisher. When he broke clear over a ridgeline, I noticed that his body sharply undulated in an almost serpentine fashion. I knew then that I had something unusual.

The very next day, I went to the Watertown Zoo, where I knew I would find a pair of wolverines kept in a three-acre enclosure. A friend, Sue Collins, went to one end of the enclosure and drove the wolverines back and forth in my direction for almost ten minutes. There was no doubt this was the creature I had seen the day before. In my elation, I immediately thought of the two contrasting biblical tenets in play in the situation, "Oh, ye of little faith," and "Seek and ye shall find."

Another anecdote I recall was related to me by Mark Brown, a DEC biologist based in Ray Brook. Mark, who is best known for his research on martens in the Adirondacks, was in the middle of a discussion concerning wolverine sightings. All of a sudden, he recounted an interesting notation he had come across while perusing the wildlife records of one of the large, privately owned Adirondack preserves. When he brought the note to the attention of the representative of this private park, which had been instrumental in the release of elk, wild boar, and moose at the turn of the 20th century, he was suddenly asked to leave the premises and not come back. When I asked if he had uncovered any mention of wolverines in their game-release records, Mark said I should ask the question upon his retirement in five years. Mark has been retired now for a number of years; and though I have often pondered revisiting this issue with him, I have not yet done so. Perhaps some day!

Several months after the sighting I made, I was involved in another event connected to wolverine sightings, which took place at a conference sponsored by the Wildlife Conservation Society. During a break in the proceedings, I informed Ken Kogut, DEC wildlife manager in Ray

Brook, of my sighting. No sooner had I said this than a wildlife technician from the DEC came forth in a burst of energy proclaiming that my sighting added further credence to his theory that "green groups" were releasing predators all over the park, and this would make their fourth sighting this spring, including one by a forest ranger. While the possibility certainly cannot be ruled out unequivocally, I doubt seriously that this rumor has any basis in reality. For starters, credible reports and sightings of some of these predators have been around now for at least six decades.

Whatever their origin, the persistence of these magnificent predators in the 21st century Adirondack landscape is fitting testimony that fact often trumps fiction.

Wolf

Since publication of *The Great South Woods*, there have been a number of developments concerning the issue of wolves in the Adirondacks and the northeast in general. For one thing, it is now usually accepted that we are dealing with two different species of wolves locally. The theory was first advanced by a group of Canadian scientists and geneticists just before the turn of the 21st century. More segments of the wildlife community appear to be concurring with this theory, though it has not yet been peer reviewed.

According to the theory, one of these wolves conforms to the typical gray wolf, as usually described. The other wolf sounds like the old Algonquin subspecies of gray wolf, which is now accorded the same full-species status as the Eastern wolf; it has been given the name of *Canus lycaon*. The latter species is indigenous to North America and split with the coyote lineage approximately 300,000 years ago. The gray wolf is a more recent immigrant from the Old World, arriving in the New World during one of the recent glacial epochs. According to this theory, the gray and Eastern wolf partition habitat by preying on moose and white tail deer, respectively. All this is in agreement with James DeKay's *Zoology of New York*, written around 1840. DeKay, official New York state zoologist at that time, stated that there were actually two different kinds of wolves in the Adirondacks. His description of the two canids revealed that one conformed physically to the gray wolf, while the other was a carbon copy of *Canus lycaon* as we know him today.

The existence of the Eastern wolf locally is in accord with the dead canid that was shown to me at Dart Lake (as recounted in *The Great South Woods*), and agrees with the statement made by DEC Lieutenant Kring to the St. Lawrence County Environmental Management Council that two "Algonquin wolves" were killed in St. Lawrence County. I always harbored a premonition that it would be my privilege ultimately to personally glimpse one of these splendid creatures in the wild, and eventually that stirring day did come.

I had just finished leading a tracking outing at the Adirondack Park Agency Visitors Interpretive Center in Newcomb. We were traveling north on state Route 30, approximately five miles north of Long Lake, just as the sun was going down, when I heard my companion, Sue Collins, cry out, "Coyote!" I turned the vehicle around and looked approximately 100 feet to the east where, on a totally exposed beaver pond, two of the most magnificent canines it had ever been my privilege to see stood looking at our vehicle with an apparent mixture of apprehension and curiosity. They appeared to be the size of deer, and I shouted to Sue, "They're *wolves*, not coyotes!" She then informed me that's what she had said first, but that I had the radio on and could not hear. The two canines then leisurely loped away, all the while glancing back in our direction. They were like no coyotes I had ever seen, no matter how large. While the setting sun could distort the coloring, to a degree, there was no doubt there was a liberal amount of reddish color suffused throughout their frames. The shape of their heads was linear yet huge, not "blocky" as in the case of a gray wolf. All in all, here was a classic Eastern, formerly "Algonquin," wolf. The relative fearlessness they exhibited toward humans, as well as their curiosity, distinguished them from coyotes. I wondered if they, rather than the coyote, were not the ancestors of the domestic dog.

While all this was occurring on the Eastern wolf front, the gray wolf was not content to rest on his laurels either. In 2002, an authentic gray wolf sighting in the southern Adirondacks was confirmed by the United States Fish and Wildlife Service in a most unusual fashion. The animal was shot by a coyote hunter while it was allegedly running with coyotes in Saratoga County. When turned in to the DEC sub-office in Warrensburg for tagging before being mounted by the shooter, the 85-pound animal was chock-full of venison. Personnel at the Warrensburg office refused to tag the animal, claiming it was not a coyote; but they did write a letter stating the animal was a wolf-dog hybrid, thereby enabling the canine to be turned over to a taxidermist for mounting. After this was done, the hunter took his bounty back to his residence for display.

There the matter rested until a wolf enthusiast from the state of Maine viewed the remains and alerted the United States Fish and Wildlife Service that, in his opinion, they were those of a wolf. A USFWS officer, accompanied by a DEC officer, then confiscated the specimen and submitted it to two different laboratories for genetic testing. The results from each were identical: The animal in question was definitely a gray wolf of probable Midwest lineage. Further tests performed by the USFWS corroborated this, also indicating this canine evinced no evidence of ever having been in captivity.

The response of DEC to this incident was predictable: The canine in question was an escaped or released pet. Al Hicks of the Endangered Species Unit informed me there was no way a gray wolf could make it to the Adirondacks, although he wouldn't be surprised if there were some Eastern, or Algonquin, wolves present here. Interesting!

The federal government has released new regulations essentially proclaiming the wolf has now recovered and should be removed from the endangered species list. In essence, this would also have the effect of abandoning any intention or effort to restore the wolf to its rightful place in the Northeast.

A lawsuit was filed by several environmental organizations attempting to rescind this federal effort at declassifying the wolf by claiming that effective wolf recovery could only be demonstrated when breeding populations had been restored over a major portion of their former range, something not yet achieved. Here the matter currently stands; what the courts eventually decide will have a significant effect in determining the future of wolves in the Adirondack Park. Regardless of the decision, however, it is apparent that wolves of both species will continue to disperse into the Adirondacks, with the Eastern or Algonquin wolf coming in greater numbers but also being subject to further hybridization with coyotes. It is obvious that a favorable decision from the courts will greatly facilitate the wolves' comeback.

Whatever the decision, I have an innate feeling that the howl of the wolf will once again become a part of the regular sounds of the Great South Woods.

Canada Lynx

Continuing reports of lynx sightings are being received on a fairly regular basis. Sightings by two recently retired DEC employees, Officer Dick Matzell and Assistant Forest Ranger Nate Jeffries, appear especially credible.

In addition, I came upon a set of Canada lynx tracks in the Cranberrry Lake Wild Forest in March 2002. I followed the tracks; but they finally eluded me by going into the thick, impenetrable conifer thickets of Peavine Swamp. The reports, although somewhat sparse, come regularly.

Photo by Uta Wister

A well-hidden lynx takes a rest.

The High Peaks were the original focus of the Canada lynx reintroduction effort conducted by the SUNY College of Environmental Science and Forestry in 1989. For a long time, the effort was believed to be a failure because of a perceived lack of reports in this area. I have, however, received a number of quite credible reports from the High Peaks area of sightings that occurred a decade or so after the 1989 reintroduction effort. Among them were several clear sightings made on outings of the North Woods Chapter of the Adirondack Mountain Club. Two lynx were also spotted by SUNY Canton professors. The teachers got quite close to the cats, who were romping in the moonlight. Both the ADK and SUNY sightings occurred higher up on the slopes of the High Peaks, where there is a plentitude of hares to provide sustenance for the lynx.

The High Peaks region itself might not be of sufficient expanse to support a lynx population without recourse to adjoining areas. In fact, a recently published continent-wide survey of Canada lynx revealed that lynx are very wide-ranging. This study also disclosed that populations on the periphery of the lynx range — in areas like the Adirondacks — are an integral part of that range and perhaps even vital to the survival of the populations as a whole. Thus, the Adirondacks would appear to be of international importance in the conservation of Canada lynx.

The ESF lynx reintroduction project was deemed by many to have been a failure, primarily due to the high number of road kills of the widely ranging cats as well as the lack of documented reproduction among the introduced lynx. The high amount of road kill could be explained by the innate tendency of large carnivores to wander extensively, and perhaps also to the fact that the Yukon Territory of Canada, where they originated, remains mostly roadless. There, it was rumored, the trappers employed to furnish the lynx had sometimes captured baby lynx from their dens and raised them in captivity. As for the lack of documented reproduction, this may be much more difficult to verify in an area with large roadless expanses, like the Adirondacks, than in still-wild areas that are laced with at least secondary roads. This latter is the situation in Maine, where proof of lynx presence and breeding has recently been documented.

Also documented in Maine has been the fact that the crossbreeding of Canada lynx with bobcats has occasionally produced hybrid beasts. At present, I am not aware of whether these hybrids are "viable," in terms of breeding, or not. If they are, this could be an obstacle to the maintenance of lynx populations in areas where the ranges of the two cats overlap, much as the possible interbreeding of Eastern wolf and coyote will have to be considered.

The elusiveness of the lynx, as well as other large felines, was graphically illustrated recently by the efforts of the Wildlife Conservation Society in its quest to ascertain their presence in the Adirondacks. The search was based primarily on feline scent markers, positioned to lure any feline within range to deposit hair or other parts of their anatomy so it could then be analyzed for DNA to identify them. An intensive search produced no Canada lynx — but, as Ray Masters and I informed investigators at a meeting of the board of directors of the Residents Committee to Protect the Adirondacks, no evidence of bobcat was ever uncovered, either. Could anything attest further to the furtiveness of felines than this?

Elk

The update on the elk situation since the first *Great South Woods* book is quite brief and not very encouraging. An environmental impact study was proceeding in a number of Catskill-area towns that had come on board in favor of the reintroduction. Those of us in the Adirondacks who were chagrined that our area was passed over in the restoration effort, for social (read political) rather than ecological reasons, were encouraged that our area would be next in line after the Catskills.

However, a new impediment has put in an appearance. The DEC has cancelled all Catskill initiatives, citing a fear of chronic wasting disease, which is transferable under certain conditions from one cervid to another — in this case, white-tail deer and elk. So far, the two confirmed cases in New York State have been in domestic deer. The department says, however, that it wants to prevent the spread of CWD to wild deer. That is fine, but it must be pointed out that there are wild herds of elk certified free of the disease, from which stock may be had.

I have heard a few cynics say that DEC has never wanted elk and is using the CWD threat merely as a ploy to thwart restoration efforts. I certainly hope this is not the case and that, in the not-too-distant future, elk will take their rightful place among the fauna of the Great South Woods and the rest of New York State, as they have recently done in a number of other eastern states.

Conclusion

What can account for the continued sightings of large carnivores in the Adirondacks down through the years? I do not ascribe to the "green-release" theory. The logic of conspiracy theories has always eluded me; and besides, considering the longevity of some of these credible reports, such a conspiracy would have to have been maintained over the last several generations.

There is another theory, a wildlife-management dictum called the "minimum-viable population theory," which posits that when wildlife numbers hit a certain low, they cannot recover and will commence a slow slide to oblivion because of demographic factors.

I can't help musing, however, on the possibility of these ultra-secretive predators persisting at extremely low population levels for extended periods of time. They may be aided in this effort by the ability of wide-ranging carnivores to communicate with each other over great distances. A graduate student could put together a good doctoral thesis by contrasting this idea with the minimum-viable-population theory. Apropos this, it is well to keep in mind that the Adirondacks never lost its deer population, unlike most of the rest of the East, with the exception of northern Maine. There has always been plenty of prey here for these predators in time of stress. In addition, the amount of old-growth forest in the Adirondacks has been variously estimated at between 300,000 and 500,000 acres, considerably more than the cumulative total for the rest of the eastern states. These old-growth areas were only peripherally and lightly trammeled by man, and they furnished ample areas of security for the "creatures of the shadow." When viewed from this perspective, it seems unlikely that some of these shadow creatures did not, in fact, survive to greet the 21st century.

I feel quite strongly that pragmatism and common sense should dictate the state of New York's response to these glorious life forms. First and foremost, stringent protection should be accorded to all of them; but the protective regime should not be disruptive of the social fabric of the Great South Woods. Cougars should be designated a game species, with no open season, while dispersing wolves, of either species, should be protected as a "non-critical population." This latter term proscribes the illegal taking of the species, while at the same time ensuring that the draconian side effects contingent upon the federal "endangered" designation is not implemented locally. The wolverine and lynx should also be put under one of the umbrella designations.

Hopefully, common sense will prevail; and populations of these creatures of the shadow will increase, so that they may be enjoyed by a broad spectrum of Adirondackers and visitors alike.

Two Fawns

Photo by Sarah and Adam Kuenzler

Photo courtesy Natural HIstory Museum of the Adirondacks

The author prepares to lead a snow-tracking guided tour.

2
THE WAY THAT I WENT

It all began with the Big Woods of old Flushing. This was a fenced-in, mature woodland adjoining farmland owned by the New York City Department of Education in rapidly urbanizing Queens after World War II. By the mid-20th century, this patch of the planet had become a green oasis in a sea of concrete. As a young boy, I had an almost mystic fascination with this area and haunted it in my spare time as I endeavored to learn its secrets. Foremost in my mind, even at this early age, was a burning desire to identify and know everything of a faunal and floral nature that made its abode in that isolated island of wild nature. I still can vividly recall, even across the years and the miles, the bounteous numbers of ring-neck pheasants and cottontail rabbits who inhabited that precious piece of the past. I now realize the populations of these species were at a saturation point that mainly reflected the absence of predators nearby.

During my tenure with the New York City Police Department, there was a brief interlude when I was able to become acquainted with and monitor what is now the federal Jamaica Bay National Wildlife Refuge. Created under the tutelage of a Park Department horticulturist named Herb Johnson, the refuge was a wildlife sanctuary run by New York City. In 1966, I got to know Johnson and his assistant, known only to me as Barney, when I was assigned to the Queens County Youth Squad of the police department. Barney called on me on a number of occasions because he had difficulties with poaching and illegal dumping in the refuge. These transgressions, often committed by juveniles, gave me a golden opportunity to learn about the wildlife at the refuge. Two of the more prominent members of the wildlife community were bobwhite quails and exotic jackrabbits. The quail, once native to the area, had been re-introduced to the refuge, while the jackrabbit had escaped from a shipment at nearby JFK International Airport. The bob-white, alas, is gone today; while I hear the exotic jackrabbits still main-tain a presence on the periphery of the refuge. The Big Woods of Flushing is today no more, having been obliterated by the expansion of Queens College; but, fortunately, the Wildlife Refuge exists today and is ably administered by the National Wildlife Service. Although I did-n't realize it at the time, this was the beginning of an odyssey into nature that would culminate in the Adirondack Park.

That odyssey gained momentum when I proceeded to Schoharie County, west of Albany. That's where my cataloging of local flora and fauna began in earnest, although I still spent pleasant October days afield in pursuit of cottontail rabbits with my Uncle Dennis Spillane, his son, Sean, and his son-in-law, Eddie Walsh. Because Dennis had an excellent pack of beagles, our pursuits were usually successful. My mother actually learned how to cook rabbit from her sister, Kitty, so her first-born son could enjoy the spoils of these efforts.

Tug Hill came next. This was not only my introduction to the North Country; it was also where I first began to tentatively describe myself as a naturalist while I sought in earnest to inventory anything that grew, flew, swam, crawled, or walked on the huge tract I had pur-chased at the top of a hill. To help defray the taxes, a hunting club was started here; and, thus, serious deer hunting came to the fore for the first time. While my stewardship ethic was now being formulated, I still felt strongly that private-land stewardship was the exclusive way to go. I inaugurated diverse private initiatives to protect the land here and, as a result, was chosen Lewis County Conservationist of the Year in 1974, as was detailed in the first volume of *The Great South Woods*. My time of advocacy was now close at hand.

That advocacy dawned shortly after I purchased my house in the town of Fine in 1974. While I continued to hunt, first becoming a member of the Weller Pond Hunting Club and, later, the Cranberry Lake Hunting Club, my thoughts turned more and more to protecting the natural treasures of the Adirondack Park. Ultimately, my hunting became confined to the Forest Preserve, as I affiliated with a base camp set up deep in the Aldrich Pond Wild Forest by the Kerr family. (They were generous enough to invite me along as the only non-family mem-ber.) Although venison was prized, the viewing of wildlife and the other natural splendors of the Creator were cherished just as keenly by the members of this rustic camp. Gradually, my outlook evolved into a holistic appreciation of the total landscape as I began to study all the components of that landscape to find out how they interacted with each other. The protection of that landscape for posterity now became paramount in my thinking.

By the early 1980s, I had begun to affiliate with different groups striving to actively protect the local environment in diverse ways. The first group I joined was Citizens to Save the Adirondack Park. This was a hands-on-group formed by Clarence Petty in response to the spread of the mammoth second-home housing developments that, at the time, were beginning to rear their ugly heads in the Adirondacks. The group disbanded as the threat of second-home development receded due to economic factors and the vigilance of the Adirondack Park Agency.

Around this time, I also authored *A Trail Guide to the Northern Adirondacks* for the Adirondack Mountain Club, and for a time I was on their statewide Conservation Committee. I am still a member of the Laurentian Chapter of ADK, and I occasionally lead a hiking expedition for them. I cherish the friendships I made in the two decades I've been a member.

The fledgling Residents Committee to Protect the Adirondacks was the next group with which I affiliated as my odyssey progressed. RCPA was formed by Adirondack residents to give support to the much-maligned Governor's Commission on the Adirondacks in the 21st Century. Governor Cuomo had established that commission in an effort to further protect the Adirondack Park, but its work was strenuously assailed by pro-development interests who tried to give the impression that Adirondack residents only cared about economic matters and were not interested in the environment. The formation of the RCPA was our way of rebutting the developers. I was one of the founding members of the RCPA board of directors, and I am still on the board today, although there was a short interlude when I was not.

Some exciting times occurred in the first few years of RCPA's existence as we held a series of open public meetings throughout the Park in an effort to galvanize support for the Park's protection. These meetings generally showed considerable support within the Park for our position, but they also brought forth detractors. On a few occasions, those opponents of the Adirondack Park became quite loud and boisterous, but they were unable to really accomplish anything, since they were definitely in a minority at our meetings.

It was also around this time that I began an association with the Adirondack Park Visitors Interpretive Center at Newcomb, where I started the monthly nature walks that I continue to lead to this day.

The VIC attempts to interpret the natural background of the Adirondack Park both to locals and tourists. My walks have accommodated both groups, in approximately equal numbers, down the years. These walks have also resulted in a number of firm friendships and have provided an excellent opportunity to get to know people from all sections of the Park.

The non-profit Indian Creek Nature Center was established on 360 acres of land leased from the Department of Environmental Conservation in the state's Upper and Lower Lakes Wildlife Management Area. The primary purpose of the group is to provide conservation education to the schoolchildren of St. Lawrence County. I have been a member of the center's board and have regularly led nature hikes for them for almost two decades. I strongly believe that education about Earth's natural order is vitally important for the development of today's youngsters, for they will be the ones called upon to preserve our environment for posterity.

The path I was unabashedly pursuing in support of environmental progress then branched into several other directions. Since 1986, I have been a member of the Governor's Open Space Committee. During the 1990s, I was also a member of the St. Lawrence County Environmental Management Council, which functioned under the aegis of the county legislature. Clarence Petty was also a member of these committees. After Governor Pataki announced the historic deal protecting all 145,000 acres of the Champion Paper Company's land in St. Lawrence County, an esteemed member of that county's legislature took it upon himself to proclaim to the Watertown Times that Clarence Petty and I "decide what lands the state of New York should steal from the people of St. Lawrence County." The paper not only printed this assertion but also chose to highlight it in one of their columns. This ludicrous assertion brought chuckles to anyone with even the remotest sense of how the state goes about purchasing land. Considering the way some hunting club members felt about losing their leases on the Champion lands, we were perhaps fortunate that we received nothing more than threats after this claim was published.

The latest effort to promote environmental awareness with which I have become affiliated is the splendid new Natural History Museum of the Adirondacks, now nearing completion in Tupper Lake. For the past several years, it has been my pleasure to lead focused natural history hikes for them in various areas of the western Adirondacks.

Speaking out in favor of an environmental perspective has not always been universally popular, and there have been times when I have done so with a certain degree of trepidation. I felt strongly that the environmental position had to be presented, and I did so even at the occasional expense of facing a hostile audience. Such an audience was very much present at a public forum in Ogdensburg, where I spoke in favor of a proposed Federal Wildlife Refuge for the St. Lawrence Valley. Actually, to describe that audience as merely hostile would be an understatement. The New York State Farm Bureau had vigorously spearheaded opposition to the refuge, and the audience reflected that view. They were quite raucous, verging on the disorderly, especially when I spoke. I felt fortunate in leaving that hall without having received physical harm.

Hostility of a different stripe was evinced when I sat on a citizens committee set up in conjunction with re-licensing the federal hydropower project on the St. Lawrence River. I was representing the St. Lawrence-Adirondack Audubon Society on the committee, which was considering all aspects of the re-licensing issue, including a proposal to return lands now owned by the New York Power Authority to local towns for development. Since the power authority, a state agency, had owned the riverfront land for over half a century, it was actually de facto parkland. I objected to exchanging those wildlands and wetlands along the river corridor for a landscape of condos and "McMansions." One of the town supervisors who sat on the committee took exception to my view. Whenever I got up to make a statement, this worthy person would give an exhibition of his musical ability by emitting a chorus of vocal twittering that, I suspect, was supposed to represent a bird chorus.

Another path that I have pursued over the past few decades has been the tracking of large, cryptic predators in the forests of the Great South Woods. My fascination with these creatures was not restricted to a feeling of awe inspired by their power and grace. It extended to a respect for their position as essential components of the Adirondack ecosystem. They are, in fact, keystone species; as such, they contribute vitally to the integrity of their ecosystems. Down through the years, I have catalogued and investigated reports of these magnificent predators from all over the Adirondack Park and the North Country. They definitely have a purpose here, and until their presence becomes biologically viable, the Park's ecosystem will lack an integral cog.

Similarly, the American beech and American elm must be fully restored to the Great South Woods in order to maintain that ecosystem's integrity. Their demise, and that of the American chestnut near Lake George, has generally been overlooked; but now the time has come, I feel, to rectify that neglect by restoring all three to their respective niches in the Adirondacks. The biodiversity boost that would ensue from their restoration defies description. Each of these forest giants has its own specific insects, fungi, lichen, and mosses, all interacting with each other and with other creatures of the forest.

All these initiatives are a fulfillment of the advocacy philosophy that underpins my view of the natural order. I believe strongly that the earth is God's handiwork and that, accordingly, we are called upon to be good stewards of this earth. While scripture talks about the spiritual realms of other "heavens and earths," there is only one planet that completely supports our existence in the here and now about which we must be concerned. The preservation and protection of this planet is a sacred trust bestowed upon us.

The Christian tradition speaks of "the integrity of creation." My belief in that concept is why I have come to have a special interest in biodiversity. Everything was created for a reason, and for that reason alone. I feel strongly that it is incumbent upon us to strive vigorously to ensure that no element of creation ceases to exist because of our actions. No finer inspiration exists for this mandate than the story of Noah in the Old Testament.

I also feel strongly that most Christian churches of today are somewhat remiss in their efforts to care for Mother Earth, some more so than others. One ancient church that was exemplary in caring for nature was the Old Celtic Church, which expired officially in the 7th Century but whose heritage I have in my genes. My interest in that heritage was rekindled by my repeated visits to Ireland, the land of my parents, during the three-year period of 1996-1999. I became acquainted with the wild, gloriously barren Beara Peninsula of southwestern Ireland, from which my father hailed. The beauty of its mountains, lakes, bogs, heather, and remnant oak woods resonated deeply within me, revealing more than anything else why the Adirondacks exert such a pull on me.

I continue on my path toward knowledge and advocacy. The quest for knowledge is pure joy, but the path of advocacy has, on occasion, been lined with both thorns and roses.

Some local residents don't view protection and preservation of landscape and species as a worthy endeavor, and they spare no opportunity to proclaim this. To these folks, the bottom line — often the only line — is the dollar, and preservation of the Creator's jeweled handiwork is of no account to them. Consequently, some of my neighbors view me in a less than favorable light, a fact that has made my life anything but dull over the years.

Still, considering the magnitude of the importance of protecting the Lord's landscape and the dire consequences to humanity if we destroy our environment, I can safely say that I have not regretted for even a nanosecond going "the way that I went."

Our gift from the Creator: All creatures great and small

Photo by Sarah and Adam Kuenzler

Were these the "good old days?"

Packing it out.

Photos courtesy Wanakena Historical Society

3
FOOTPRINTS IN THE FOREST

OLD-TIME WOODSMAN

Among the early settlers are those who literally and figuratively left their footprints in the forest primeval. There were, of course, others who came before them. Since we know very little about the original Native American inhabitants of the area, however, we must start with the European pioneers of the area and their descendents.

Most I did not know personally, but there are a few I did. Some of these were official New York state guides, while others were not. Due to the remoteness and relatively late settlement of our area, guiding as a profession lasted longer in the Great South Woods than in the rest of the Adirondacks.

All of the woodsmen who followed left indelible marks on the area, marks that a keen observer can discern to this very day. There were other notable woodsmen whose presence graced this forest as well, but constraints of time and space prevent me from mentioning them all.

FIDE SCOTT

Uncle Fide (also known as Philo) is probably the most well-known of these woodsmen. Fide Scott was the prototype for Silas Strong in Irving Bacheller's famous turn-of-the-20th century novel, *Silas Strong, Emperor of the Woods*.

Fide was born in Jefferson County and came to the frontier town of Fine somewhere around the time of the Civil War. Fide established his domicile near the hamlet of Fine in an area that subsequently bore his name. Here he spent the winter months. He became known for the excellent quality of the maple syrup produced from his sugar bush.

It was the break-up of winter and the advent of spring, however, that sent the blood coursing through Fide's veins. It was then that Fide packed a seven-month supply of provisions on the back of a cow and proceeded to walk eight miles back into the trackless forest until he reached Big Deer Pond, where he and his pet dog would be in residence until the onset of winter.

Big Deer Pond, which was originally named Lost Lake by Verplanck Colvin, was at that time on land belonging to a timber company. The company ostensibly employed Fide as a caretaker to watch over its deserted cabins, though one can only guess what they had to be "watched" for in this remote location. What is not conjectural is that "Uncle Fide" had the time of his life hunting, fishing, and trapping in his own little corner of the world. When the time came that the proverbial frost was on the pumpkin, Fide packed his provisions and, with dog and cow, proceeded back to the haunts of man to spend another winter.

Big Deer Pond is today the middle leg of the Bog River-Oswegatchie River canoe trip. Stop there, listen intently, and you can feel Fide's presence here even now.

George Muir

George Muir is another of the old-time woodsmen whose name is still renowned. George's fame rests mostly on a particular avocation he pursued after New York state, around 1870, put an official bounty on the two large predators then present in the Adirondacks: the cougar (or panther) and the wolf. The cash bounty paid by the state was $20 for a panther and $30 for a wolf. George hunted the two with equal gusto and accounted for a total of 39 wolves and 39 panthers, which was more than the total accumulated by all other bounty hunters combined.

George hunted these splendid creatures when snow was on the ground in winter. He would snowshoe tirelessly until coming upon the track of one of his quarries in the snow, whereupon he would release his dogs to chase the animals until they were either treed or brought to bay. George would then dispatch the animal and present it to the local town clerk for documentation and payment. Recently, a noted wildlife biologist has suggested that George's figures could have been inflated by presenting the same carcass or parts thereof to different town clerks. George's descendants, who still live locally, vociferously deny this, and I have a tendency to believe them.

In later years, George was the caretaker of a camp in remote Gull Pond, where he tragically met his demise through exhaustion while snowshoeing the 14 miles back to it one April day in the early 20th century. This tragic ending to the exciting life of an old-time woodsman is graphically detailed in Herbert F. Keith's book, *Man of the Woods*.

As the cougar and wolf return to occupy their ancient haunts in the Great South Woods, I like to feel that the spirit of George Muir is present still and nodding in approval.

Skip Lansing

I first became aware of Skip Lansing in conjunction with a 60-pound bobcat he had supposedly harvested near Wanakena around 1950. Ross Morgan, a Vermont forester, relayed the tale to me while we were talking about my home area. I was duly impressed and decided to pursue the matter. I discovered that Skip Lansing had indeed harvested a monstrous-sized bobcat at that time, which very well could have tipped the scales at 60 pounds. If true, this definitely would be a world record as far as I know.

Skip Lansing was one of the graduates of the New York State Ranger School who returned to work in the Great South Woods. For a period of four years, though, he was a silviculturist with the Green Mountain National Forest in Vermont. When he came to Wanakena, he raised both mink and foxes on commercial ranches. He also guided hunters and fishermen, but it was mostly as a trapper that he excelled. Many other local trappers benefited from Skip's expertise, which he freely shared. Skip spent much of his time at his rustic camp on the Oswegatchie River near the Plains. It was a heart-wrenching experience for him when he had to take the camp down in conformance with the State Land Master Plan.

Skip was also something of a naturalist and wrote copiously of bird and mammal life and their changes over the decades. He also was enthused with duck hunting along the Little River near Heath Pond and wrote of his experiences there. These notes of Skip's were never published, and his family retains them to this day.

Skip detailed the demise of the fabled local brook trout and concluded that the former New York state Conservation Department was primarily culpable by allowing beaver populations to become too abundant before establishing an open season on them. He also indicted the presence of motorboats in the Oswegatchie River; while generally dubious of the Adirondack Park Agency, he agreed with them in their banning of motors on this river.

He was definitely a woodsman for his time and one I definitely regret having missed meeting by a short length of time.

Fay Welch

An old-time woodsman that I feel a special affinity for is Fay Welch. Fay wore twin hats as both a naturalist and a hunter and, in addition, was an avid hiker who had once been a governor of the fledgling Adirondack Mountain Club. His empathy, extended to all three of these endeavors, is something of an uncommon trait among woodsmen.

At first, Fay Welch was a student at the State College of Forestry at Syracuse, where he later became an instructor. His father, Jim, first brought him to Cranberry Lake at a tender age. Jim Welch was a noted otter trapper and a respected guide. Fay later followed Jim into guiding, but, in addition to the orthodox guiding for deer hunting, Fay Welch also took parties on nature jaunts through the forest. On these expeditions, he shared his intimate knowledge of the local flora and fauna.

Like Skip Lansing, Fay Welch kept nature notes and a diary. Some of the nature notes were incorporated into a chapter in the book, *Cranberry Lake: From Wilderness to Adirondack Park*, edited by Albert Vann Fowler. Fay writes wonderfully of getting lost with Wilfred Morrison, another guide, while leading a group of clients to look for Fide Scott's old camp on Big Deer Pond.

As in the case of Skip Lansing, I regret arriving in the Great South Woods just a few years too late to personally meet Fay Welch. Nonetheless, the spirits of both linger in these big woods to this very day.

Mike Virkler

Mike Virkler, who hailed from Croghan, was one old-time woodsman I did get to know. I had the pleasure of spending some time with Mike at his leased hunting camp at Buck Pond, where the west branch of the Oswegatchie River begins its flow to the St. Lawrence and ultimately to the ocean. During Mike's tenure, his camp was on land belonging to International Paper Company. Around 1986, the land was sold to the state of New York and has become the Watson's East Wild Forest.

The camp that Mike had inhabited for decades was dismantled in accordance with state mandates. It was transported to the Adirondack Museum at Blue Mountain Lake, however, where it was re-assembled and placed on display to give an indication of what a typical Adirondack hunting camp looked and felt like. Thus, generations of tourists and residents will get to see a cultural artifact of the Great South Woods that is slowly fading away.

I spent some time with Mike at this camp and greatly enjoyed the times when Mike expanded on the times of old in these woods. This was a definitely enjoyable learning experience for me. Among other things, I learned how nearby Hog Pond received its name. It seems that pigs were kept by loggers at this remote location as a ready supply of meat. One night, a storm blew down the fences of the enclosure where the swine were kept, and the pigs ambled merrily off into the forest. They led a feral existence in the nearby vicinity for several years, until finally they were shot out. Their brief tenure in the area was reason enough to bestow a name on one of the headwater ponds of the west branch of the Oswegatchie.

Mike was famous among the other camp lessees of the Oswegatchie for his feeding of meat scraps to both martens and Canada jays in winter. I was personally privileged to witness up to nine Canada jays and two martens present at the same time. It was a sight I will forever treasure, as I also will treasure the opportunity of getting to know Mike Virkler.

Doran Johnson

Doran Johnson, of Fargo and Wanakena, can well be said to be one of the very last of the old guides. I was fortunate enough to encounter Doran (also known as Red) almost immediately upon my retirement from the New York City Police Department. Subsequently, we spent a considerable amount of time together for the next several years. Red was, in a sense, a mentor who introduced me to the ways of the woods and wild lands of the Great South Woods.

For many decades, Red hunted and trapped the most remote reaches of the Oswegatchie River above Wanakena. That first summer, Red and I spent three blissful weeks exploring the far reaches of the river corridor and beyond. Ostensibly, this was in preparation for a fall trapping and hunting foray, which ultimately we did make. But, along with the scouting itself, there were wondrous observations of all the myriad parts of creation that the Lord had placed in this magical river and environs. Birds, mammals, trees, flowers, fish, insects, herptiles all were looked at with respectful awe; and each was indelibly impressed in our spirits. Although Red was a veteran hunter and trapper, he also had a reverence for the wilderness that is not often matched either in today's nimrods or in the non-consumptive users of the land.

When motorboats were banned on the Oswegatchie River in the

1970s, Red adapted to the new order as if he had been born with a paddle in his hands. I still vividly recall one of his witticisms apropos of this new order: "When you paddle upriver, the wind is always in your face; and when you come back downriver, it's still in your face!" How true it is, considering all the dramatic curves the Oswegatchie makes in its winding course.

In reminiscing, Red spoke fondly of the old guiding days of Wanakena, and he enhanced my life by sharing these memories with me. He also recalled trapping for a full season with fabled Adirondack hermit Noah Rondeau back at Noah's shanty on Cold River. This was way back in the 1930s, and it was the scene of Red's first cougar sighting. Subsequently, he saw another one at Toad Pond back in the Five Ponds Wilderness. Red also told me how all the local guides had opposed the construction of the gravel road (truck trail) to High Falls during the depression years. This was done by the DEC in conjunction with the Civilian Conservation Corps of the federal government, ostensibly to expedite fire-fighting efforts in the vicinity. The guides viewed this as a make-work effort that would only detract from the wilderness aura of the area. Red was, therefore, quite pleased that the "truck trail" was reverting back to a wilderness path by the 1980s in accordance with the State Land Master Plan.

Red trapped mostly water mammals: beavers, otters, and muskrats, with the occasional mink. Disaster struck one year in the late 1980s when all his muskrat sets along the river, from Inlet to Cage Lake Springhole, were methodically pilfered, both for fun and for the traps. This so discouraged Doran that he left the Oswegatchie forever and went over to the Raquette River to trap the next year. He did this for only one year before finally hanging up his traps in the 1980s.

His spirit, though, is still on the river — and in my heart.

Some Other Woodsmen

Constraints of time and space preclude me from including many other old-time woodsmen who graced the Great South Woods in this brief discourse. Prominent among those not included here are Art Leary and Wilfred Morrison of Wanakena. Both were prominent guides who are mentioned often in articles about the Great South Woods as well as in Herb Keith's fine book, *Man of the Woods*. In addition to guiding, Art Leary and his wife, Bessie ran a boarding house in Wanakena that catered mainly to sportsmen and outdoor enthusiasts. Wilfred Morrison, who at various times had different camps along the river, which he used in his guiding, was described as having a fascinating French-Canadian brogue that reflected his Scotch-Irish heritage and francophone culture. His arrest by Game Protector Homer Duffy and subsequent trial for deer jacking have become legends now of Wanakena.

There is another Wanakena woodsman who has not been publicized as much in print as the former duo. Yet, when I asked Red Johnson who he considered the best woodsman of all, he answered without hesitation that he thought it was George O'Connor. I later got to know George's son, Rory, an expert woodsman himself. George, and later Rory, maintained a camp beyond High Falls; and I learned much about their escapades there in my lively conversations with Rory.

Cranberry Lake also had many notable guides. Two of the foremost were Barney Burns, who plied his woods lore at Brandy Brook, and Irish-born Bill MacAlesse, who later opened a popular restaurant near the hamlet. Then, too, we must not forget that Cranberry Lake was also the haunt of Frederic Remington and Irving Bacheller. While these two renowned individuals rose to fame, primarily in the arts, they received their inspiration from the primeval forests of the time of their sojourn here.

All of these, and countless others, left their footprints in the forests of the Great South Woods. I like to feel that their spirits, too, still grace these woodlands today.

A successful hunt

Photo courtesy Wanakena Historical Society

Old boundary-line markers between Hamilton & St. Lawrence Couties

Old Trails

In addition to the marked hiking trails maintained by the DEC in our area, there are a slew of other trails that are essentially unmarked, although some of them were marked, at least sporadically, in the past. They are pathways through the forest that in times gone by probably felt the tread of the feet of most of the woodsmen previously listed.

The origins of these pathways are varied, although most began in some fashion as a way to harvest the bounty of the Great South Woods. Usually, they created a route to a lake or a favorite hunting area and then led the hunter back to the settlements in an expeditious manner after he had secured the sought-after fish and game. Some of these trails are informally kept open by hunting parties to this day. One of the trails was used by early farmers to secure fodder for their livestock, while another was constructed as part of a military operation. Finally, the blow-down of 1950 and its aftermath resulted in the creation of one of these trails.

Leary Trail

Noted Wanakena guide, Art Leary, with the help of Wilfred Morrison, built the Leary Trail in the early 1920s. It was an officially marked DEC trail until the blow-down of 1995 devastated it so completely that it made any restoration expensive and futile. Accordingly, it was deleted from the last Five Ponds Wilderness Unit Management Plan, published after the blow-down.

It originally made a loop after leaving the High Falls Truck Trail and then rejoined that trail after approximately three miles at a point opposite Round Hill Rapids on the Oswegatchie River. It was here that Art Leary had his guiding business and guided his clients, often with Wilfred Morrison.

The trail proceeded in an up-and-down fashion and probably passed by as many beaver ponds as it was possible to pass in a distance of three miles. There were exotic Douglas fir trees all along the trail, and their presence and identity proved to be quite a puzzle to decipher, for a friend and for me. The beaver ponds furnished many wildlife sightings during the period of more than two decades when I utilized the trail. Especially notable were the sightings of great blue herons, wood ducks, otters, and, of course, the beavers themselves. More bats were to be seen here than along other trails, and these included the only sighting I've ever had of a silver-haired bat. I definitely miss the Leary Trail!

Dobson Trail

The Dobson Trail never reached the status of a marked, official trail. It remained an informal "herd path" through the forest for its entire tenure.

Bert Dobson constructed it early in the 20th century as a means of reaching the elegant sportsman's camp he had established at High Falls. The trail branched off the High Falls Truck Trail to proceed almost due south along a low point between Little and Big Roundtop mountains before reaching the Plains. From there, it re-united with the truck trail to go the short distance to High Falls.

The Dobson Trail was also obliterated in the blow-down of 1995. A short segment of approximately a quarter-mile has been re-established by a hunting party that maintains a campsite along it during the autumn hunting season. This trail, like several others, owes its continued existence to the informal maintenance of various public hunting groups that have established temporary "camps" as bases for hunting and trapping during the fall season.

One of my most cherished memories of the Dobson Trail is following close upon the heels of a black bear that preceded me on the trail as it dug up the roots of the yellow herb, adder's tongue, as it ambled along. I finally rounded a bend, and there he was! Fortunately for me, fear conquered him before he could conquer me, and he exited the scene at a rapid pace. Of course, I can never forget that it was the fastest route to High Falls from Wanakena.

Old Hay Road

This old trail owes its origin to early farmers in the town of Fine who created it to gain access to bluestem and other wild grasses growing in the marshes along the outlet to Big Otter Pond. These wild grasses were utilized as hay, providing emergency fodder for the farmers' livestock until the forest could be cleared and planted closer to their farmsteads. This was primarily in the vicinity of the hamlet of Fine, where the farmers had brought their cattle from the northern part of St. Lawrence County to settle the area.

Trudging along this old trail was like recapturing an intimate vignette of a hallowed past. This trail also proved very fruitful in producing sightings of wildlife. These old trails are, in general, usually much more conducive to wildlife sightings than the marked DEC tails, probably because of a scarcer human presence here, and perhaps, too, the narrower width of the path. Deer are sighted in far more abundance; even the occasional red fox and coyote can be spotted, which are almost never seen along marked official trails. I would go as far as to say that the larger mammal species have a definite tendency to habitually avoid official marked trails, preferring the unmarked paths where they appear to be far less wary. My most evocative wildlife sighting along the old Hay Road was that of two adult beavers meticulously grooming each other on a point of land adjacent to a beaver flow. They never knew I was present.

The Old Hay Road, of course, led in later years to an illicit hunting camp that stood for decades, defying the minions of the law. The 1995 microburst signaled the end of the Old Hay Road, just as it did many of the other unmarked paths through the forest. The microburst has not obliterated my memories of the Old Hay Road, however, nor of the cryptic hunting camp that was once its destination.

Triangle Trail

The Triangle Trail is one with a unique twist to its story. While several trails were destroyed by blow-downs, the Triangle Trail was, in a sense, created by one: that of 1950. It happened in the following fashion.

The New York state Attorney General's Office issued a judgment at that time saying that hurricane-felled trees in the Forest Preserve could be harvested, despite Article 14 of the state constitution. Accordingly, log roads were built through the forests to take out the fallen timber. The Triangle Trail had its beginning in such a fashion.

The trail received its name because it created a triangular strip of land adjacent to the Inlet Flow. Local folks from Wanakena bestowed the name; they also proclaimed that the triangle created was the scene of some of the most productive deer hunting drives in the Great South Woods.

While the Triangle Trail had its origin in one blow-down, it was obliterated completely by another. The microburst of 1995 rendered the trail impassable for a while, but the trail has now been restored for three-fourths of a mile — approximately half of its original length. The two tiny, jewel-like bog ponds at the foot of the esker that the trail traverses are still reachable, as are the occasional huge specimens of virgin white pine, which occur as solitary trees in several places along the route. Once glimpsed, these towering trees are not easily forgotten. For me, they define the trail, as do the pairs of screeching ospreys that construct their nests in the upper reaches of the behemoths' crowns.

Red Dot Trail

The fledgling Adirondack Mountain Club constructed the Red Dot Trail in the 1920s, under the guidance of A.T. Shorey. In many areas, it followed the pathway of an unmarked route utilized by sportsmen, referred to as the "Fur, Fin and Feather Trail." The Red Dot Trail was meant to link Stillwater Reservoir with Wanakena, but at no time was it marked continuously for the entire route.

Today, there is a marked trail from Stillwater Reservoir extending approximately four miles or so to Salmon Pond and passing by several other lakes in the process. Salmon Pond is the domicile of several unique fish species, including lake trout and lake chub. A little past Salmon Pond there previously existed a rare natural habitat similar to the Oswegatchie Plains near High Falls. This was quite singular to the area and is referred to as a "boreal heath" by scientists. The one existing here by Salmon Pond is now much filled in, but a keen observer can still discern its features.

The Red Dot Trail passed near High Falls, about halfway along its route. To me, High Falls evokes memories of the radio-collared moose detailed elsewhere in this book, as well as the fearless woodland jumping mice frequenting the campsite at night in an attempt to filch leftover food from beguiled campers.

Now long consigned to obscurity by the rampant forces of nature, the path can still be distinguished in a few places today by a focused observer. Terry Perkins, the retired ranger at Stillwater, has traversed the entire route of the trail from Stillwater to Wanakena on a number of occasions.

He has also recently guided a number of individuals along this route. The utmost of navigational skills are called for in this endeavor, however. From my point of view, it enhances the allure of the Great South Woods that an area exists where such a feat is still possible today.

ALBANY ROAD

The Albany Road was built around 1811, primarily to move military equipment to the vicinity of Ogdensburg, on the Canadian border. This was on the eve of the War of 1812, and the road was intended to extend from Sacandaga to Russell. Like the Red Dot Trail, the old military road was never doable all at one time. It was done mainly in segments. Still, 30 years ago, when I first became acquainted with these wonderful woods, I occasionally found remnants of the old roadbed; and there was even a much-tattered DEC sign proclaiming the "Albany Road." The sign probably dated from the 1940s, and the last time I saw it was approximately two decades ago.

Still standing are parts of an old canon near Oven Lake, deep in the Five Ponds Wilderness — so we know that something of its military function was, in fact, achieved. The second objective in constructing the road was to spur a local population explosion. Fortunately, this was an abject failure at the time.

The road, after entering the town of Fine, crossed the Oswegatchie River a little south of High Falls. It then re-crossed the river at the established ford at Inlet. This Inlet crossing apparently acted as a magnet for early inhabitants of the region. Indian arrowheads, usually quite rare in the Adirondacks, have even been found here. Fred Griffin, the ranger at High Falls, was quite knowledgeable concerning the Albany Road and shared that knowledge with others around 50 years ago. Clarence Petty, who was Fred's supervisor, regaled me with a few tales about Fred. Although I did not get to meet Fred, fortunately I got acquainted with his brother and two sisters before they passed on to the other world.

The Albany Road was an interesting artifact whose time has long passed in the Great South Woods. Yet, on certain select days back in the forest, an attentive listener can still feel its resonating presence.

OTHER OLD TRAILS

There are a number of other old trails that covertly snake through the forest preserve, usually on their way to clandestine hunting camps. They were probably begun by the early guides and, since their demise, have been assiduously maintained by modern sportsmen. I have followed some of these trails in the Raquette Boreal Wild Forest and the Grass River Wild Forest for a distance of several miles. They have long been a feature of the landscape, and I do not begrudge their presence here.

Most of these trails are unnamed, but one that does have a name is the Old Post Henderson Trail. This trail proceeded from the Post Henderson mill in Star Lake into the forest for at least seven or eight miles. It was originally built to transport timber to the mill, but later it was utilized by the old guides, mainly in their pursuit of hunting and fishing activities.

The beginning of the Old Trail is off limits today, due to posted land and beaver flooding. Segments of the trail, however, are being utilized today as part of the Alice Brook Snowmobile Trail and the Boundary Trail to Cage Lake. Both of these pathways are maintained and marked by the DEC.

All of these trails, and others, are an integral part of the history of the Great South Woods. They are form a direct link between the old guides and our modern sportsmen and hikers, perpetuating the ancient, timeless cycle of life in these hallowed woodlands.

Photo by Nadine McLaughlin

Photo courtesy Wanakena Historical Society

Strange happenings in the Great South Woods.

4
TALES OF THE WILD

INTRODUCTION

In a heavily forested landscape like the Adirondacks, where much of our wildlife is nocturnal, coming upon sightings of some of our more elusive residents of the wild is a rare treat indeed. How much more of a treat it is when one of these creatures is encountered in the actual process of interacting with other members of their clan, or even with a different species entirely.

Over the years, I have been privileged to witness a fair share of these "interactions." The following is an account of some of the encounters the reader may find of particular interest. In addition to the encounters with wild fauna, I have also listed a few incidents with people who probably could also be described as wild. I list the episodes alphabetically here, rather than picking which of these short tales are the most unusual or interesting.

BIGFOOT FAKER

It was a call I knew eventually would come. It was from a reporter with the *Albany Times Union* who wanted to know if I had acquired any knowledge of Bigfoot in my rambles in the Great South Woods. It was sometime in 2001, about a year after the first *Great South Woods* book was published. I imagine this was where the reporter got her inspiration to contact me.

I pondered the implications here. It would be so easy just to reply in the negative and have the matter extinguished before it really began; but, in fact, I had acquired some knowledge of "Bigfoot." Moreover, because, since childhood, I have never been able to lie without experiencing sleepless nights immediately afterwards, I reluctantly related to her the occasions when my paths and Bigfoot's had crossed.

The encounter was on a very humid June afternoon around 1990 when the black flies were at their horrendous worst. I had just returned from a round-trip hike on the Burntbridge Pond Trail, east of Cranberry Lake. I was sitting in my car at the trailhead parking lot, detailing the locations of recent blow-downs along the trail on a map, which was to be sent for publication in *Adirondac* magazine. There were perhaps a half-dozen vehicles in the parking lot when an individual alighted from a vehicle at the furthest side of the area and proceeded along the trail holding what appeared to be a large foam coffee cup. This, and the lack of hiking attire of the individual, piqued my curiosity somewhat. It was the height of the fly season, and he was decked out in shorts and an undershirt and was hatless. I shrugged to myself and continued with my notes. When he returned to his vehicle after approximately 15 minutes, the man apparently noticed me for the first time, for he gave an involuntary start before seeming to quickly recover, then rapidly got into his vehicle and drove off. I did not need my past career's training to tell me that here, indeed, was something that didn't meet the eye properly. My curiosity thoroughly aroused by now, I exited my car and walked up the trail the man had just left, which I had just walked down a half hour earlier.

Within 200 feet, I came upon a series of huge, vaguely human footprints in the mud of the trail, each approximately 15 inches in length. I recall counting eight or nine of them before they abruptly disappeared. These tracks had definitely not been there before. What this individual had in the "coffee cup" now became crystal clear. What is not clear is what was transpiring in his tortured mind when he laid down this fraud in the mud of that trail.

Robinson River Buck

Opening day of the 1981 big-game season found my companion and me settled in at Camp Johnny, an officially designated campsite on the upper Oswegatchie River above High Falls. Camp Johnny is nestled at the foot of a ridge still crowned with an impressive stand of old-growth white pine, despite its having been partially decimated by the blow-down of 1950.

As well as a hunting trip, our trip was also to be a trapping foray for my companion; so when we left camp early in the morning to paddle upriver, we were also checking his mink sets. As I recall, my companion was delirious with joy at finding no less than 11 minks in his sets.

"My best day in 20 years of trapping," he delightedly proclaimed.

Just as we arrived at the confluence of the Oswegatchie and Robinson rivers, a magnificent eight-point buck stepped out on the banks of the Oswegatchie. Apparently we both saw the deer at the same time, just as he got his first view of us. What occurred next was indeed most wondrous. This noble buck stayed right where he was and inserted those imposing antlers of his into one of the alders that lined the riverbank. My partner and I both looked at each other with astonishment before he proclaimed, "With an IQ like that, he shouldn't be left in the gene pool." With that statement, the Robinson River buck met his demise.

When we got back to the settlements and Dave Allen's store in Cranberry Lake a week later, we found out the deer weighed 225 pounds, field dressed. A DEC representative, while checking the deer's dentition, estimated his age to be four years. All in all, the buck made quite a trophy.

Questions that arise from this encounter: Was the unusual reaction of this buck to us prompted solely by blind passion? (His neck was bulging, indicating he was near the peak of his rutting) Or could it possibly be that, at that very remote location, we were the first human beings he had laid eyes on?

Trout at Graham Pond

Graham Pond is a medium-sized body of water nestled among low hills in the town of Pitcairn. It is (or was) teeming with brook trout, and it was zealously guarded against trespassers. I can personally attest to these two facts from the one time I was present at the pond.

Before my present period of enlightenment, I would occasionally stop off at a neighborhood pub to quench my thirst. The Greenwood was one such establishment at the time. I stopped there one day almost 30 years ago, after finishing a difficult tour of duty in the Big Apple the day before. Dick, a friend who lived locally at the time, was present in the pub and suggested we leave immediately and proceed to nearby Graham Pond in pursuit of brook trout. I was instantly amenable and said so to Dick, but I also added that I was under the impression Graham Pond was posted. Dick smiled at me and proclaimed he knew the owner.

The shortest access from Route 3 to Graham Pond is by way of ascending a rather steep cliff. Dick decided we'd go by horseback, despite the fact I had never been on a horse in my life until then. He took his

Photo courtesy Wanakena Historical Society

Stringing a good line

horse from a pasture at the side of his house and procured another family horse for me. Thus equipped, we started on our trek up to Graham Pond.

I was thoroughly surprised when all went well on our trip, and we arrived at Graham Pond in due fashion. At the pond, all was serene and glorious. The fishing lived up to my partner's raving, and we had secured close to our maximum allotted number of fish when a vehicle drove up to the other end of the lake. Dick instantly announced that the vehicle heralded the arrival of "old man Graham" and that it was time for us to vacate the premises without delay.

I was flabbergasted at this sudden turn of events and reminded Dick that he had told me he knew the owner. Dick turned to me and, with a completely straight face, said, "I do know him — but he hates me."

I was a trifle annoyed, to say the least, as this put me in quite a vulnerable position. To receive a citation or summons would have repercussions in my employment in the New York Police Department. We proceeded back down the cliff in record time and eventually arrived safely at Dick's house. That we did so was due either to mere fortunate chance or to the intercession of a few guardian angels. Anger and irritation on my part quickly faded, and Dick and I enjoyed a good laugh at the proceedings. He subsequently moved to Canton; and we lost touch for a while, as is the way of life.

This tale has a sequel, however. About 20 years after the incident, I became aware that my old friend Dick had purchased a diner on the outskirts of Canton. I dropped in one day while his wife and daughter were working in the diner. I introduced myself and related the tale to them and asked them to pass it on to Dick to see if he remembered. There was an immediate reaction that could best be described as astonishment from them. It seems Dick had regaled quite a few with this tale over the years, and there were even some cynics who believed it was merely a fabrication on Dick's part. My appearance in the flesh bestowed the mantle of authenticity to the tale.

Dick and I subsequently renewed our old friendship; and on days when there is a lull in the diner's activities, we relate the story to anyone present whom we consider worthy of hearing it.

High Falls Moose

There is another ungulate tale revolving around the Upper Oswegatchie. The locale for this story was High Falls, where its pair of lean-tos makes it a wilderness junction for hikers and paddlers. The protagonist was a female moose named Alice who had been outfitted with an electronic collar by university researchers in Newcomb. Alice stayed put around Newcomb for a number of years before inexplicably commencing to wander. Therein lies the tale.

I received a call from Ray Masters, a research biologist at Newcomb, who stated that Alice was now at High Falls, according to their electronic tackling. Would I like to go with him to check on her? After an enthusiastic assent, I proceeded to the DEC boat launch at Cranberry Lake, where I joined Ray, along with two forest rangers and Al Hicks, mammal specialist with the DEC Endangered Species Unit. From there, we went to Jenack's Landing on Dead Creek Flow, thus shortening the usual trip to High Falls by approximately four miles.

This was a year or two after the blow-down, and the area around High Falls presented a picture of utter desolation. As one wit had recently proclaimed, "The highest objects now standing are the two lean-tos," this in an area where previously majestic white pines had stood sentinel.

Now, fallen trees were piled in every direction, creating an impassable landscape everywhere off the trail. Ray had his electronic device on, and we could clearly hear the moose blundering through that impenetrable maze, sometimes no more than 50 feet away. Strain as we would, however, I recall that only two of us actually claimed to see it. I was not fortunate enough to be one of those two. After several minutes of frustration trying to glean at least a glimpse of this mightiest of cervids, we gave up and went back to Cranberry Lake.

This tale does not end here. How that moose did winter! Being monitored electronically, she apparently traveled right down the Oswegatchie River. Numerous sightings were also made of her around Wanakena, Gouverneur, and Ogdensburg, then across the St. Lawrence and into Canada. After several more months had elapsed, the radio signal stopped working (no more movement) right smack within the confines of Algonquin Park, the huge provincial park that has been paired with the Adirondack Park. It was here that Alice met her ultimate demise.

I learned two lessons from this tale: First, the proposed Adirondack-to-Algonquin Wildlife Corridor has definite possibilities. Second, rivers are also vital to the safe passage of wildlife.

A Garter Snake, a Toad, and Me

Over the years in my woodland rambles, I have noticed that most species of prey are either very quick and nimble or else they are camouflaged very well. Those that are not either are often toxic to the taste of predators and quick to announce it with bright coloration as a warning. Monarch butterflies and red efts spring readily to mind here. The American toad does not possess such warning coloration but does make himself very obvious as he plods along woodland trails. He is indeed toxic to animals, but not, apparently, to snakes. I acquired this knowledge firsthand while grouse hunting nearly three decades ago.

It was classic mid-October Indian summer weather with grouse lying low and refusing to flush. I heard a rustle off to my side and upon casting my gaze there observed a large garter snake in the process of swallowing live an agitated, medium-size toad. The toad was half-way in the snake's mouth and imminently set to disappear down his gullet.

I could visualize the toad's feelings of terror (if, indeed, amphibians have feelings) and, instantly filled with righteous outrage, I promptly blew the snake to smithereens with my shotgun. The toad exited the mouth of the snake but remained seemingly paralyzed in a state of shock. For 20 minutes, the toad remained in this torpor-like condition. Eventually, when he did not respond to my prodding, I left the scene, leaving him to his fate.

I have often pondered this incident over the intervening years. When I do so, a sense of shame and remorse overwhelms me. A hard lesson was absorbed that day, one that stayed deeply imprinted in my psyche. It mainly concerns my recognizing the importance of the cycles of nature, and acknowledging the predator's important role in that cycle. I see both as being securely in the grand design of the Creator.

Bobcat, Creek Chub, and Me

We can all agree that the bobcat is among the most furtive of creatures, as wily and cryptic as a feline can be as he strives to seek out his elusive prey. I have seen only three bobcats in my Adirondack rambles, but the sighting that I remember most vividly took place not in the Adirondacks but at an isolated camp on the top of the Tug Hill Plateau. This sighting, which was my first of a bobcat, came about in a truly amazing fashion.

It was a pitch-black May evening at my camp back in the woods of the town of Montague. The camp, which was at least three miles away from any permanent human presence, had a small creek passing approximately 50 feet from it. Shortly after dark, I was alone when I heard loud, persistent splashing coming from the creek. When I went down to the water to check on the sounds, what unfolded before my eyes was a truly wondrous spectacle. Dozens of creek chubs were churning up the water in a primordial frenzy of mating. I stood entranced, watching them from the middle of a storm "dam" I had created of flat shale rocks placed across the narrow creek. The chubs remained entirely oblivious of my presence.

I stood on the stones, so absorbed by the scene I was witnessing that I apparently lost track of time. Suddenly, I became aware that I was not alone. I turned and uttered a spontaneously inane, "What are you doing here?" to the creature I instinctively knew was beside me. With that, the creature bolted and ran up the banks of the creek, giving me a quick view of his posterior by the light of the propane bulbs outside the camp. That quick glance seemed to say "bobcat" but, as my flashlight was not working, I had to wait for morning, when there would be tracks in the mud of the creek banks, to be sure.

At dawn, my anxiety knew no bounds as I bolted from the camp to see what was going to be revealed on the banks of the creek. The suspense quickly dissipated, for registered there on the bank were two quite clear tracks of a large bobcat. There was no doubt about it. The only lingering speculation regarding the cat's presence right there beside me on the stone dam was how long he been beside me before I noticed him.

I don't know the answer; but as for the reason, I have to assume the cat was more pragmatic than I and was just there for a meal. Or is it just possible there might be a pinch of validity in that old proverb, "As curious as a cat?"

Bears at High Rock

As might be expected, I have had many encounters with black bears over the years. The one that looms largest in memory occurred around 15 years ago, at High Rock on the Oswegatchie River. Its sequel only a year ago was so poignant that it left me shaken emotionally.

Brent and Gaylord Kerr and I had paddled upriver to the vicinity of High Rock, where we hoped to get in a spot of fishing. We were lighting a campfire for lunch when I spied what I thought was an out-of-place stump perhaps 100 yards away in the midst of the vast alder swale and boreal marsh that stretched out from under us as we lunched on top of High Rock. I pointed this out to Gaylord, who was quick to reply that

Bears, bears, everywhere in the Great South Woods

Photo by Uta Wister

the object of my focus was a bear, not a stump. His brother Brent quickly added his assent to that statement.

Just then, the "stump" rose, and we were greeted with a most wondrous sight: a huge black bear standing upright, like a primate. After what appeared to be an eternal interval, he dropped back down onto four legs and continued rooting in the marsh again, as if we were of no further interest to him. It now appeared we were of no significance to him at all.

He resembled, both in size and aspect, the Alaskan brown bears that are so frequently depicted in film and print. All three of us were convinced that it was, in fact, the largest bear we had ever laid eyes on. For me, it was also a vivid message that the reading glasses I was wearing up to that time were not going to suffice much longer.

The sequel to this tale unfolded in 2003, when I went to pay my last respects to Brent. The end of his time in this world was imminent, and as I entered the house, his wife and sister-in-law asked me to tell him to "let go." Brent was still waging a valiant struggle against the cancer that was raging through him, although he had not spoken in hours.

I spoke to him for a good while without eliciting any response, a distinctly one-sided conversation, as I rambled on about moments in life we had shared. Then I came to the incident at High Rock. I related it to Brent and then asked him a question: "I guess you don't remember that, fellow?" The entire room hushed as he responded in a firm, positive voice, "Yes, I do." After this, his first utterance in hours, he lapsed back into silence.

It was with dewy eyes and all choked up that I took my leave. I'll have to wait for the next world to see my friend Brent again.

A Collie, Carrots, and Venison

These three may appear to be an unlikely trio, seeming at first glance to have scant chance of having even the most tenuous of connections. Yet, the paths of this trio did in fact cross approximately 15 years ago in a most unusual fashion. I was an integral part of the occurrence and recollect it vividly to this day.

I have always maintained a garden of some sort at my house in the town of Fine. The sandy loam soil there is ideal for root crops and potatoes. That year, I had planted potatoes, beets, and carrots. The carrot leaves, and even the tops of the carrots themselves, were being decimated by deer that usually put in an appearance after dark, in spite of the fact that I had a large buckwheat patch nearby expressly for them.

It was early afternoon of a mid-September day. I left my son Kieran's collie dog, Falcon, tied up outside while I attended to some business inside the house. (I had inherited Falcon, so to speak, when Kieran and his mother and sister moved from Armonk in Westchester County to an apartment on Roosevelt Island off Manhattan.)

I heard a burst of barking outside, but thought little of it at the time. The next thing I heard was a heavy pounding on my front door. Upon opening the door, I found two young males standing before me. One of them excitedly said that a "bunch of deer" were in front of my house. I also detected the sweetish odor of marijuana, with which I was well familiar with from my police days, on the breath of the individual who said he was the driver. They asked to use my phone to notify authorities of the accident. ("What accident?" I thought.) When that was done, we went outside to assess the situation.

I immediately observed two dead deer on the side of the road. I told the driver that I knew of a needy family in Fine that could use the meat. I figured they would not be interested in the meat, since they had told me they were urbanites hailing from Rochester. To my surprise, however, the three strenuously protested, stating they deserved the meat, due to the damage inured to their pickup truck. At that time, I told the driver about the odor I detected from him and suggested he "chew some gum or something" before the troopers arrived.

When the police did arrive, I gave them an outline of what had happened, and the trooper left to inspect the tire marks. The driver of the car then pulled me aside and said, "You know your friends, the needy people in Fine? Well, I think they should have the venison." After the accident report was prepared, the trooper informed us that a DEC conservation officer was on the way and would issue a permit to keep the venison. After my friend from Fine arrived, a search of the surrounding area revealed the carcass of a third deer approximately 100 feet off the road. Presumably, it had managed to stagger there before dying.

Three dead deer from one vehicle collision! Something I had not heard of up to that time, nor have I heard of it since.

Over the years, I have often pondered this incident and the inadvertent part I played in its occurrence. In retrospect, it appears that the deer — a doe and her two yearlings — arrived early that September afternoon to commence feeding on the carrots. The barking of the collie may have startled them, and they apparently bolted in panic across the nearby highway. The excessive speed of the vehicle was no doubt a factor also.

An unfortunate episode indeed, but one that did bring with it a slight silver lining in the form of venison for a family that certainly appreciated it. It also provided an affirmation of the old axiom that, occasionally, fact is indeed stranger than fiction.

Two Guys from Brooklyn

I was sitting in the Oswegatchie Diner when a call came over the two-way radio mentioning two hikers lost between Star Lake and Wanakena. Something seemed to resonate inside me upon hearing this. After all, I helped write the hiking guide to this section (the Adirondack Mountain Club's *Adirondack Trails: Northern Region*, edited by Peter O'Shea, Duncan Cutter and Neil Burdick), so I have some proprietary interest in the trail.

It seemed the two hikers had started in Wanakena at the High Falls truck trail and intended to arrive at the trailhead to the Boundary Trail in Star Lake in three days. They had arranged for a friend to pick them up at the juncture and ferry them back to Wanakena. When they failed to appear for the rendezvous, they were declared missing; and a search procedure was instituted.

Listening to a little voice deep inside, I proceeded to the trailhead on Young Road, where the hikers had planned to rendezvous. I arrived there late on Sunday afternoon and found that the DEC had temporarily called off the search with the intent of resuming it early Monday morning. As there was still some daylight left in the long July day, and as that little voice within was still active, something propelled me along the trail.

I recalled an alder-spruce swamp just off the trail, perhaps a half-mile in, where I had been seriously turned around last year. I arrived at a point where a cliff overlooked almost the entire swamp, and I commenced to shout. I had no sooner done so when someone called back!

For the next several moments, we played musical chairs while the person in the swamp kept moving as he called back to me. Due to the thickness of the mostly conifer canopy, we had no visual contact. Finally, I hollered harshly to him to stay put and took a compass reading to his position. I was then able to get to him and bring him back to the trail.

The subject was a young, physically fit male who was quite agitated and not in the least grateful that I had found him. He berated the ADK hiking guide as being the cause of his getting lost. Finally, I could brook no more and told him so.

After he had become more placid, he informed me that his hiking partner had collapsed from fatigue and was two miles farther up the trail. He had left his partner there with instructions to stay put while he continued on the trail to secure help. He informed me that he and his friend were both gym teachers at a private prep school and were from Brooklyn.

When we arrived back on Young's Road, I took him to the home of the McGuinness family, where he received aid while I notified Search and Rescue of the situation by phone. As I deemed this an emergency situation, with time being of the essence, I asked the McGuinesses to go with their all-terrain vehicles (ATVs) up the verboten trail and bring the second hiker out. They readily complied and were able to successfully retrieve the other hiker, none the worse for wear, on the back of their ATVs.

The second hiker recovered rapidly and was quite normal by the time the state police arrived. He was also much more reasonable in demeanor than the first hiker and definitely grateful for being rescued. He relayed to me what was perhaps the clincher to this episode: His ill-mannered companion, who had still not expressed any thanks for his rescue, did indeed live and work in Brooklyn. This was by no means, however, his genesis. He was actually born and raised in Gouverneur!

I gleaned two more life lessons from this episode: 1) not everyone who says he's from Brooklyn actually is; and 2) little voices from within that remain persistent should not be discounted lightly.

Fish tales and tall stories abound in the Great South Woods.

Photo courtesy Wanakena Historical Society

5
EXOTICS

INTRODUCTION

Exotics are those species that were not originally native to the Adirondack Park before the advent of Europeans. Their arrival in the region was due, either directly or indirectly, to the advent of man upon the scene. These alien species disrupt native ecosystems in many ways, most of them negative.

The Adirondack Park is unusual among the regions east of the Mississippi in possessing relatively few of these exotics. The extensive forests and wetlands of the Adirondacks have retained their basic integrity of species to a degree generally not seen elsewhere in the East.

This does not mean the Adirondacks have been completely free of such species, either in the past or present.There have been several interesting cases where mammals have been introduced to the Adirondacks, have flourished for a while, and then gradually faded away. Some still retain a nominal presence, mainly on the periphery of the park or around human settlements.

The Adirondack Park has remained even more a bastion of native integrity when it comes to exotic plant species. The ecosystem of the Adirondack Park has remained relatively intact, preventing these nuisances from establishing a foothold, even though they have become ubiquitous elsewhere. In addition to displacing native species, recent studies have shown that a prevalence of alien plants reduces the biomass of the entire ecosystem. This comes about through a decline in the local insect population, which is generally less well adapted to feeding on these alien plants than it is to consuming native species. As insects are a fundamental part of the food chain, there is a corresponding decrease of other species and their numbers right up that chain.

Several exotic insects are now common in the Adirondack Park. Some of these are widespread and well known, such as honeybees. Members of an alien species of lady beetle have taken it upon themselves to infiltrate the older houses of the region during winter. The seemingly ubiquitous cluster fly, also probably exotic in origin, has exhibited a similar pattern.

Other exotic insects are less well known, and their invasions are probably localized. One such invader is the European hornet. Most species of earthworms have now been similarly shown to be European in origin.

The species I have listed in this chapter are diverse and interesting, and they have equally diverse and interesting explanations for their presence in the Adirondack landscape.

WILD BOAR

This old-world animal is an unlikely candidate for inclusion in a treatise about the Adirondacks. There is, however, a definite connection between this native of European woodlands and the Great South Woods. While somewhat checkered, that connection certainly prevailed in the past and might even exist at present.

Around the turn of the 20th century, wild boars were released in a number of the large, private estates then existing in the Adirondacks. The primary purpose of these liberations was to establish boars as a game species, since they are highly esteemed by local **nimrods.** Within a short period after release, many of the boars escaped and established a wider presence in the Adirondacks at large.

The vicinity of Tupper Lake was one area where the boars were abundant, and they retained a presence in that general area at least until the 1940s. The fact that they were rightly given no protection in New York state, due to their status as an exotic species, probably was the main factor contributing to their ultimate demise. I have a hunch that the heavy snows of winter that generally prevail here was also a factor in their failure to establish a permanent presence. By mid-century, reports of the presence of boars had generally ceased.

Then, unexpectedly in the 1970s, a number of wild boars were shot and killed by local residents around Indian Lake. It is unknown whether these were recent releases or remnants of the original six or seven, introduced decades before. Experts who examined the slain animals stated they appeared to be of genuine wild boar lineage rather than feral domestic hogs.

The next chapter in the checkered local history of the wild boar was to take place in the St. Lawrence Valley, near Canton. Environmental Conservation Officer Dick Matzell informed me that an off-duty state trooper had shot and killed a wild boar that was harassing his domestic pigs. Dick investigated this and found out another wild boar was shot several miles away and taken to a local meat packer for processing. It was presumed both of these animals were escapees from one of several local private hunting preserves.

Next, we fast-forward to April 2004, moving to the woodlands of the Indian Creek Nature Center near Canton. Roger Hutchinson, a member of Indian Creek's board of directors, was walking the nature center trail when he and a companion spotted a huge wild boar a short distance ahead on the trail. Roger, who is a retired senior forester for the DEC, was successful in snapping a wonderful photo of this. I subsequently went to the area to look for the boar, or any sign thereof, but my efforts met with mixed results. I did not see any boar or their distinctive tracks, but I did observe some spots where a boar might have been rooting about in the shrubbery.

In September of that year, a wild boar was reportedly run over by a vehicle on Hannawa Falls Road, adjacent to the nature center. Again, like the animals in 2000, it was presumed that this boar had escaped from a local hunting preserve.

So the situation stands today. In neighboring Vermont, wild boars that have escaped from similar hunting preserves have become so numerous in the central part of the state that conservation officials are considering establishing a hunting season on them. Could this scenario happen here? It certainly is plausible, especially in the St. Lawrence Valley. Even without the establishment of a viable population, there will likely be continued escapes from private hunting preserves.

Keep a sharp eye while walking the woodlands of the Great South Woods. There could be a surprise or two just ahead on that trail!

Ring Neck Pheasant

Tame, confused, and forlorn, they appear suddenly from June onwards along the roadways of our area. Many succumb in collisions with motor vehicles, as they appear to have a mortal fascination for prancing along these roadsides. They are ring-neck pheasants, and various 4-H and game clubs have probably released them recently, in conjunction with DEC.

The birds rarely over-winter in our area. The striking plumage of the male bespeaks their exotic origin. Despite their alien background, I have a grudging affection for them and take delight in seeing them. That affection is in total contrast to how I usually view exotic species, especially in the confines of the Adirondack Park. This is because pheasant memories reach far back into my boyhood to the time I first encountered them as an eight-year-old in Flushing, Long Island. The year was 1946, and I well remember riding my bicycle back from an altar-boy meeting at the local church. I inadvertently flushed approximately a half-dozen of these splendidly attired fowl from a wayside thicket and was thrilled to the very core of my being. There next ensued repeated trips to the local library until final identification was made. I vividly recall being hooked from that moment on by pheasants and wildlife in general.

On top of Tug Hill, the hunting club I formed in order to help me meet my tax obligations released scores of pheasants. For two successive years, the pheasants were released in the open areas of my 737 acres. The birds were released in June, but invariably they were all gone by October 11, the beginning of the small-game hunting season. How they did provide sumptuous feasts for predators galore! Foxes, coyotes, fishers, and weasels all partook of the bounty provided. Foxes appeared to be especially adept at decimating the pheasant population; but all of these listed animals were instrumental in their demise, including probably a pair of goshawks that nested not too far away. All of us agreed that, while we got no sport from this venture, we enjoyed watching the birds and even occasionally glimpsing one of their predators.

Pheasants usually cannot survive the harsh winters generally prevalent in the Great South Woods. Unlike grouse and wild turkey, they have never acquired the habit of feeding on buds in winter. They are restricted at this difficult time to seeds and insects, commodities in short supply hereabouts. I did flush a cock pheasant at the Indian Creek Nature Center in late March 1990. There was still snow on the ground. I remember thinking, as I enjoyed the awe of the bird's graceful flight, that this was the first one I could say had truly over-wintered. Unfortunately, it has also been the last I have personally observed over-wintering. My ramblings are, in the main, concentrated on the Adirondacks, rather than the St. Lawrence Valley, but surveying pheasants occasionally in the valley is not beyond the realm of possibility.

Even before the advent of winter, there are hazards impacting pheasant survival here. The gaudy, exotic plumage of the cock pheasant has got to be an attractant to predators and have a negative effect on pheasant survival. Then, too, many of the birds released seem to be semi-tame.

A ride from the Adirondack Park boundary in Fine to Tupper Lake will usually disclose a pheasant either hugging the roadside or lying flat on the road after a vehicle encounter.

An alien species, yes, but I still have to admit experiencing joy at seeing them. This joy emanates either from sentimental reminiscing or from a pure, visceral delight at their exquisite color and form.

European Hare and Hungarian Partridge

These two animals are, admittedly, a strange pair to be linked together in a chapter; but a number of similarities do exist. Both species hail from Europe primarily and were originally introduced into North America as game species.

The European hare initially established successful populations in the Hudson Valley of New York and in southern Ontario. These introductions were both private ventures. Initially, they thrived to such a point that they were considered an official game species in New York by the DEC. This was despite the fact that, almost immediately, there were problems with hare depredation on apple orchards in the Hudson Valley. The creatures are now unprotected in New York state, and their numbers have dwindled so steeply that it is uncertain now if any are left in the Hudson Valley. It is believed that changes in agricultural practices started the rapid decline in their numbers, while the spread of the Eastern coyote from the Adirondacks southward put the finishing touches on their demise. The only personal experience I have had with European hares is observing a road-killed specimen in Columbia County in the 1960s.

The Ontario population of European hares fared better and apparently even crossed the St. Lawrence River occasionally, as proven by a number of specimens taken in North Country towns adjacent to the river. My feeling is that these crossings took place over the ice in winter. According to the DEC, there have been no recent confirmations of their presence in this area.

On the other end of the river, however, two friends have recently informed me of the presence of "huge jackrabbits." Zoologist Lee Harper was doing contract ecological work for the New York Power Authority when he made his sighting, while Nancy Olsen was participating in a breeding-bird survey when she spied them. Although their "giant jackrabbits" could be just that, I believe it is a better bet that these are European hares that crossed the St. Lawrence River by utilizing the New York Power Authority islands as stepping stones. I personally have never encountered a European hare within the confines of the Blue Line; but a relatively recent book by William K. Chapman, *Mammals of the Adirondacks*, does claim they are present there.

The other member of this duo, the European partridge, was introduced to a number of areas in New York state, but its only real success story was in the St. Lawrence Valley. The partridge was ideally suited to the small-scale agriculture that once prevailed locally and, for a time, the bird established a thriving population there. My one sighting was a most memorable one that happened around 1980 while I was hunting cottontails. A small, compact flock of the birds rose up in unison amidst the swirling snowflakes of a plowed field, skimming over a hedgerow to alight in an adjoining field. A wonderful sight, but one that I have not seen again.

In a situation similar to that of the hare, numbers of partridge have sharply dwindled over two decades. Changes in agricultural practices and coyote predation are probably the culprits here also. Interestingly, in my trips to Ireland I discovered that populations of the partridge there, where it is native, were also steeply declining.

Despite this, according to the DEC's records, a few partridges seem to have managed to be recorded annually, so give a second glance to any "large pigeons" flushing in a flock from open fields. You may be rewarded with a look at partridges, instead.

Badger

This denizen of Midwestern prairies would seem to be a decided anomaly in discussing the Adirondacks and adjacent areas. Anomaly or not, badgers have a definite history in this area, as a perusal of the literature will reveal.

The literary history begins with the epic 1947 book by William J. Hamilton, *Mammals of the Eastern United States*. Hamilton stated that several badgers had "been taken" in the western Adirondacks during the 1930s.

The New York State Conservationist came out next with an issue in the 1970s listing all badgers that had been confirmed in New York since the end of World War II. These approximately half-dozen recorded sightings were scattered throughout the Adirondack Park and the area immediately to the west. State trappers targeting red fox, in an effort to stem a rabies outbreak in the 1970s, had secured a number of the specimens.

Reports continued well after that 1970s publication. The last one that I know of to definitely be published was one taken near Lake George around 1990 and mentioned in the *Conservationist*.

I continue to hear and receive reports of badgers up to the present time. While admittedly anecdotal in nature, many of them appear to be quite credible. New York State Trooper Mike Dolan gave me one of these reports. Several other local residents have also given me reports that I consider reliable, including one from a friend who, along with her ex-husband and father-in-law, sighted a badger and at first believed it to be a wolverine. When shown pictures of a badger, however, she quickly confirmed its identity. An interesting sidelight here is the fact that the animal in question hissed and spit vociferously, which is a trait often accredited to badgers.

I vividly remember one occasion, which occurred while I was giving a talk on my first book, *The Great South Woods*, before students at the Cranberry Lake Biological Station. I was approached at the conclusion of the lecture by one of the students who claimed he had seen a badger near Tupper Lake. I believed him!

While the main habitat of badgers continues to be open prairies and grasslands, they may also be found around marshes and even in open forests. This is especially so if the soil is friable and easy for digging. Gophers and prairie dogs are the mainstay of their diet but, lacking those, they will be amply satisfied with cottontails and chipmunks, which we have in abundance.

The Journal of Mammalogy published an article approximately a quarter century ago claiming that the badger had completed a natural range extension to New England at that time. Though this article was later proven to be in error, there has indeed been a more modest expansion of range into far-western New York.

This, though, does not account for the natural occurrence of badgers in our area. Where, then, do we have to look to account for their presence here?

Once again, the hand of man lies close to the truth.

Around the middle of the last century, E.J. Dailey of Ogdensburg, a noted trapper and fur buyer, was raising badger locally for the fur trade. A number of individuals who knew Daily have told me that he released all his badgers when the market for fur bottomed out in a subsequent recession. I feel certain that this, and possibly other ventures like it, account for the badger's presence locally, at least from the 1950s onward.

Are they still around? A sharp eye and keen focus might provide the answer to this query some day on a ramble in the South Woods.

EXOTIC FISH

The history of exotic fish in the Adirondack Park reveals a unique situation. Here, in the name of sport, a different set of parameters is applied to fish than the one imposed upon mammals and birds. Fish have been liberally introduced to numerous Adirondack lakes and ponds solely to enhance the quality of piscatorial pursuit. Further, many native species of fish have been moved from bodies of water where they naturally occurred to other bodies of water where they were not originally present.

This situation prevails today, primarily due to the existence of a slew of impassable waterfalls all around the perimeter of the Adirondacks. These waterfalls precluded the passage of many species of fish. Several of these species from surrounding areas were, consequently, not originally found in the upland areas of the Adirondacks. The DEC accordingly embarked on a massive transfer of species from lowland areas to the highlands, abetted in many instances by private interests. In this process of rearranging the Lord's handiwork, they completely disregarded an unusual group of mostly boreal fish that had lived here since the close of the last Ice Age. Included in the native fauna of the uplands were the following: brook trout, lake trout, creek chub, pearly dace, bullhead, two kinds of suckers, pumpkinseed, and a few others. It is a safe bet to say that their numbers have now been considerably diminished and their ranges altered. One species, the round whitefish, has even been placed on New York state's endangered species list. I know of two lakes in our region where it is present.

The main species that have been introduced successfully into the Great South Woods from the adjoining lowlands are yellow perch, northern pike, brown trout, and two species of black bass. A number of these introductions have had dire consequences; others have resulted in contentious situations.

One of the most recent was the clandestine introduction of largemouth bass into Low's Lake. The bass proliferated so successfully that what had previously been a trout water now became a Mecca for bass fishermen from throughout the East. Rather than paddle in, many of the visiting anglers elected to be dropped off at the remote location by floatplane. A thriving industry then ensued here, which many detractors claimed was detrimental to the area ecosystem, besides causing consternation to other users of the area. This situation was ultimately resolved only after a series of public hearings and the promulgation of a unit management plan that eventually banned float planes.

Then there is the case of the establishment of northern pike in Cranberry Lake, which also took place quite recently. Originally, pike were present in Lake Champlain, and probably Lake George, but were absent from the highlands. Pike are a fine game fish and are actually beneficial where trout are not present. About a decade ago, these voracious warm-water fish suddenly appeared in Cranberry Lake. Their increase was so rapid that ice fishing for them is now permitted in the winter. As to who put them in the lake, and why, that remains a mystery of the Great South Woods.

Yellow perch were released into the area at a much earlier date. After becoming established, they had a devastating effect on the local brook trout fishing, which was, at that time, famous throughout the United States. This was accomplished mostly by the perch preying on the young of the brook trout. The perch is a fine eating fish, bones and all, but this is slim consolation for the virtual disappearance of the glorious brook trout.

The brown trout was also an early introduction to the region. Generally, it has exhibited a more benign presence than the preceding trio. It is present all along the Oswegatchie River below the dam at Cranberry Lake. Sometimes, the brown trout coexists with brook trout, but usually it prefers warmer water. Another haunt of the brown is the Grass River in the towns of Clare and Russell. Streeter Lake has a good brown trout population, resulting from private stocking before New York state assumed ownership of the lake. On one memorable occasion, I was there when Brent Kerr caught a brown trout at Cage Lake Springhole — which is, to my knowledge, the furthest upriver they have been encountered.

Rainbow smelt, an anadromous species that usually leaves the ocean and ascends upstream to breed, was stocked in Star Lake as a forage fish for the indigenous lake trout. The ritual on Star Lake was for the smelt to head up the tiny inlet stream to lay their eggs. In connection with this, I vividly recall one spring day when there was a committee waiting there to greet the smelt as they ascended upstream in their mating frenzy. This waiting committee was replete with dip nets and buckets and labored industriously for several hours pulling smelt out of the water. Two things were noticeable locally after this: 1) rainbow smelt populations were much sparser; 2) a fish diet was the order of the day for a number of local families for a good number of days afterward.

Still on the subject of exotic fish, I had an interesting encounter of a cryptic nature awhile back. Friends from Wanakena called to inform me they had come upon a 33-inch fish on the shores of the Oswegatchie

River above Newton Falls. They referred to it as a "red" salmon or kokanee. After referral to several fish guides, we determined it to be a Chinook salmon. The Chinook is a western game fish that has been introduced to Lake Ontario but, so far, is unknown to our area. The DEC fisheries personnel in Watertown concurred with the identification after viewing a photo of the fish. Their prognosis was that a person or persons unknown placed it there as a hoax. My friends remain unconvinced. They relate the tale of an old-timer who claimed to have caught a Chinook in Cranberry Lake 20 years ago. Were Chinook clandestinely stocked in area waters sometime in the past, with this specimen providing evidence that they have miraculously survived? Given the aquatic habitat present locally, this scenario seems, on the surface, to be quite dubious, at least to me. But, having said that, it has to be acknowledged that stranger things have happened in the realm of nature. The kokanee referred to is also present in a few lakes hereabouts, including Twin Lakes in the town of Fine.

Finally, we come to the fish that were native to certain lakes and ponds in the Adirondacks but absent from others. This situation has, above all, not remained static; and there has been a reshuffling of native species throughout the region. Close friends of mine, with my tacit approval, have even participated in this endeavor by placing bullhead in a half-acre shallow kettle pond that had been previously devoid of fish. Brook trout, pumpkinseed, and suckers have been universally transferred from water body to water body, all in the name of sport. Even the Horn Lake strain of brook trout, a variety endemic to another region of the Adirondacks, has been placed in Bear Pond adjacent to the Pepperbox Wilderness Area.

Quite a story! Definitely more variety now, and probably more excitement, but I can't help wonder if something has been lost along the way.

Feral Dogs and Cats

These two much-beloved household pets have the potential to drastically affect wildlife population when they propogate in a wild state. They have, in fact, done so in many areas of the United States. Truly feral dogs and cats, however, have rarely established themselves in any numbers in the Adirondacks and have generally presented only a minor nuisance in that regard. The main impediment to their establishing a population here has been the inclement weather and heavy snows of winter, as well as the abundance of predators in the area.

Photo by Nadine McLaughlin

Complacent exotic.

When we consider the dog, we see that free-ranging canines, as opposed to truly feral dogs, have certainly been a serious issue here. So serious was the problem once that there was a law on the statute books stating that dogs chasing deer were subject to being shot on sight by any individual witnessing it. Certain dogs would pack up for the day, chase and kill deer, and then return to their masters at night. Worse still was the fact that, in retaining the instinct to kill, the dogs had, after thousands of years of being fed by us, lost their ability to make the killing swift and sure. Consequently, the deer suffered immensely before finally succumbing, and they were frequently eaten by the dogs while still alive. I observed this myself on one occasion during the 1970s.

This once-major problem in deer management in the Adirondacks has declined significantly with the establishment of coyote populations all through the Park. While coyotes occasionally mated with free-ranging dogs when they first colonized the Adirondacks, there is now ample evidence that they view domestic dogs as a potential competitor to be eliminated as quickly as possible.

I personally prefer the coyotes doing what is natural in the way of the white-tail, rather than domestic dogs artlessly mangling the deer and then proceeding back to the manor for processed dog chow.

House cats are continually dumped off in remote, end-of-road locations in our area as they become unwanted by their owners for various reasons. Invariably, they perish soon after. The cause of their demise is the varied array of predators at the scene, just waiting to partake of cat meat. Fishers, foxes, coyotes, and bobcats — none of them would pass up a chance to dine on this dainty morsel.

There is the occasional feline, however, that does succeed, in the face of the odds, to establish at least a semi-feral existence. Usually, they have covert access to human shelter and food. I think of one such feline who secured shelter in and under the hunting camps at Aldrich when the occupants were not on the premises. In addition to the fare of the forest, which he hunted diurnally (thereby escaping most of his predators), he also hunted shrews and mice around the cabins. Most of the time his behavior was so cryptic that humans were unaware of his existence. This included two good friends of mine who moved to Aldrich and let their un-neutered female cat outside on occasion. Imagine their surprise when their house cat returned one day, quite in the family way. One kitten from this litter was adopted by my daughter, Carmen, and became her cherished companion for almost a decade. Another of these semi-feral house cats had his domain in the vicinity of my home in the town of Fine, where he found shelter in an abandoned barn for almost two years. During his tenure, there was a pronounced scarcity of hares and chipmunks in the locale surrounding the house.

Dogs and cats are a decided blessing to man. This is especially so when they are confined to the domicile of their owners.

Exotic Flora

One aspect of nature of which the Great South Woods has a definite paucity is the range of exotic floral species. Due to the mostly unfrequented forests and pristine wetlands that are prevalent here, these troubling alien life forms have quite sparse populations in the Adirondacks. Apparently, the intact ecosystems usually prevailing in the Adirondacks present a formidable barrier to the establishment of these species.

The Adirondack Nature Conservancy has taken note of this fact and, through surveys and other actions, is actively monitoring the spread of a number of potential problem species. Prominent among these are phragmites, purple loosestrife, Japanese bamboo, Eurasian honeysuckle, and garlic mustard.

Purple loosestrife is quite common in the St. Lawrence Valley, but I have come upon it only in a sparingly few peripheral wetlands in our area. I have never noted any garlic mustard in local woodlands.

This is certainly not the case with Japanese bamboo (or knotweed, as it is sometimes called), which is not only present but apparently spreading. It seems to prefer the vicinity of roadways and the shores of rivers and streams. This plant spreads by roots and, therefore, usually appears in thick patches when present at all. It blooms late in the year and has one redeeming factor in that it provides a bounteous supply of pollen for native bees and wasps.

Another of the targeted species that I occasionally see is phragmites. This huge reed usually denotes the presence of severely debased soil. One small area where there is a luxuriant patch of phragmites was once the site of a massive oil spill near the Little River outside of Star Lake.

A target species that I inadvertently had a hand in spreading is the Eurasian honeysuckle. This fruit-producing shrub was formerly handed out by the Cornell University Cooperative Extension as a wildlife food. I partook of this largess in cost-sharing one year and planted a number of the shrubs around my house in Fine and on my acreage in Tug Hill. This shrub is usually inconspicuous, except for the very early leaf-out that it performs in spring, due to the fact that it is still on a European calendar.

Besides those species targeted specifically by the Nature Conservancy, there are a few others that I come across in my rambles. Most of these species are found in areas where the vegetation has been disturbed by man. One exception to this rule is the helleborine or European "weed" orchid, which has snugly made its home in the forests of our area. This inconspicuous member of the orchid family seems to be able to carve a niche for itself even in extensive, unfragmented forests. I see it regularly in the Five Ponds Wilderness and along the trail of the Newcomb Visitors Interpretive Center. So far, it does not seem to be inflicting any damage on the native ecosystem.

Another exotic herb that appears to still be on an old-world time schedule is coltsfoot, which displays its yellow blossoms along area trails and woodsides long before native flowers have even begun to dream about blooming. Apparently, it was introduced in pioneer times as a remedy for suppressing coughs.

Then, of course, we have the case of those annual and semi-annual herbs that proliferate along our roadsides and fields, sometimes to the exclusion of all else. These species need heavily disturbed areas to thrive, and they quickly fade as the forest takes over an area. Many were introduced inadvertently from Europe in that long-ago era when agriculture was transported from the old world to the new. Prominent among these herbs are Queen Anne's lace, chicory, ox-eye daisy, orange hawkweed, and a host of others whose varied colors enlighten our roadsides all through the growing season.

With the presence of alien tree species, we are presented with an entirely different situation. In the main, they have been unable to carve out a niche in the mostly intact forest that prevails in our area. There are two notable exceptions, which occasionally do reproduce locally. Both were initially deliberately planted after the disastrous forest fires of the early 20th century in an effort to re-forest the open areas left by the firestorms. Since many of the foresters of the fledgling forest industry of that time were European, they resorted to the use of the two European forest trees they were most familiar with. These were the orange-barked Scotch pine and the huge-coned Norway spruce. Both are now present in a number of plantations on Forest Preserve land, stretching from Tupper Lake to Star Lake. The most impressive plantations I see are in the vicinity of Axton, on the Raquette River, and near Leonard and Chandler Ponds, a few miles from Sevey's Corner. Both of these, in addition to a plantation named for him near Tupper Lake, were planted under the direction of Bernhard Fernow, who is usually considered the father of American forestry.

Both species have also become sporadically naturalized in our area and have become a minor component of the forest in a few areas. This is especially so of scotch pine in the Five Ponds Wilderness and the adjacent Cranberry Lake Wild Forest, while the stronghold of Norway spruce appears to be the Forest Preserve lands along the Tooley Pond Road.

Another exotic tree presented quite a puzzle to a friend and me two decades back before we were able to identify what it was. Gaylord Kerr, of Aldrich, and I found these unidentified conifers in an area three miles from the trailhead along the old Leary Trail, which was obliterated by the blow-down of 1995. We originally conjectured that perhaps the trees were hybrids of red spruce and balsam fir. Finally, after some research, their true identity was revealed: Douglas fir. It turns out that the trees were planted in the now-remote area back in the 1920s, when access to the scene was far easier. I must confess the two of us felt quite good at resolving this puzzle.

The alien floral species do have a presence here, albeit one that so far is truly slight and unimportant. For that fact, I am eternally grateful.

6
WILDLIFE CHANGES

INTRODUCTION

Someone once said that, with the exception of death and taxes, the only real inevitability is change. This is especially so regarding dynamic, ever-evolving ecosystems and the wildlife associated with them. In the more than three decades I have spent in the Great South Woods, those woods have savored more than their share of faunal change. Some of these changes have resulted from natural range extension of certain species, while the presence of other species was due to the intervention of humans. Still other species experienced a range contraction, or a reduction in numbers, by the occasional establishment of new arrivals.

There are also temporal changes, usually local, as species wax and wane with the advent of forest succession. Logging and farm abandonment figure both positively and negatively in these local changes to the degree that they set back succession as individual species respond to the landscape's evolutionary process.

Some change is to be expected in the natural course of events, but the changes of the past three decades appear to be unusually volatile. Within some of these changes may lie an early harbinger of global climate change about which I know very little. If it is there, it is only the tip of the iceberg (no pun intended), and strenuous and studied efforts will have to be undertaken to prevent a wildlife disaster of a magnitude that would dwarf the tsunamis of 2004. Just for a start, effective wildlife corridors would have to be established to provide for massive migration of wildlife in response to this environmental change.

Some of the species whose populations have undergone changes since my arrival on the scene are listed in this chapter. A few of these species have had their populations affected solely by habitat changes. Most, however, owe their population variations to more complex factors.

Moose

The moose is probably the most obvious topic of interest when talking about wildlife changes in the past three decades. There were no moose present when I arrived on the North Country scene in 1971. The first officially documented permanent-population report was dated in 1980, although I have heard moose were on the scene a few years before that date.

Up until then, the occasional moose who wandered into the Adirondacks invariably met an early demise before being able to even think of procreating. A trio of moose, consisting of a cow and two calves, pranced through the town of Fine in the 1950s before they all met their destinies in the vicinity of Streeter Lake.

By 1980, things were different. More moose began to arrive from an ever-expanding population in New England. Their numbers were now enough to begin breeding, which they proceeded to do ever so tentatively because of the preponderance of bulls in the population. This demographic resulted directly from the tendency of bulls to wander far more extensively than cows.

Informed sources estimate that, as of January 2005, there were between 150 and 200 moose residing in the Adirondack Park. They are now spread unevenly across the park, with populations centered in the Moose River plains, Perkins Clearing, Newcomb, and the northern Domtar lands. Although there is still something of a general imbalance, there are now enough cow moose that bull moose don't have to resort to consorting with female Holsteins, as they once did.

With the population increase, an interesting situation has arisen. Large warning signs, erected by the New York state Department of Transportation to alert motorists to the presence of moose, have a tendency to inexplicably disappear. Many are sure to have gone on to adorn fraternity houses and club halls as illicit souvenirs, but I'm not certain that something else may not be in play here also. Certain property-rights groups were incensed at the DEC's proposal in the early 1990s to actively release moose in the park. Considering the difficulty in removing the cumbersome traffic signs and their repeated disappearance, I'm wondering if the misguided hand of one of these groups may be behind the mischief — pure speculation, but who knows?

What is for certain is that the moose now present in the Adirondacks are unusually furtive and elusive, despite the fact that bulls regularly weigh over half a ton. I come upon tracks and signs of this huge herbivore fairly regularly; but as of January 2005, I've seen only two of the animals themselves. Most of them are coming from New England, either swimming across Lake Champlain or going south of the lake into Washington County. Moose also come across the St. Lawrence. In late 2004, at least three moose were present on New York Power Authority islands in the St. Lawrence River. Ownership of these islands is now in the process of being transferred to the Mohawk Nation in settlement of a long-standing land claim. One can only hope that the Mohawks will provide as good stewardship of the land as the power authority has. Knowing some of their environmental staff, and their integrity, I feel reasonably optimistic.

September and October are the height of the rutting season for moose. It is then that the normally furtive bulls commence to travel in search of cows, who have also become more active. As you watch the autumn color rising in the hardwood foliage, keep one eye aimed at ground level; you may catch a glimpse of an equally dramatic creature standing at the edge of the forest.

Red Fox

About a decade ago, my daughter, then on a visit to Ireland, purchased an enchanting tape, presenting it to me on her return to this country. As I recall, the words were in both English and Gaelic and celebrated the life of the "red prince of the moonlight": the red fox. This title is not bestowed gratuitously, for though the red fox is of moderate size, he has a definite air of royalty surrounding him.

This title brings to mind a tense moment on the St. Lawrence County Environmental Management Council, at a time when I was a member. We were discussing a pending proposal to place a bounty on coyotes in New York State. Passions were high on both sides of the issue. A respected woodsman and town supervisor who sat on the council got up and made a statement to the effect that the county's population of red fox, a noble animal, was being greatly diminished by the coyote, which was not a noble animal. While I agreed with the assessment of the fox's real majesty — and also with the supervisor's assessment of the cause of the plunging fox population — I could not in principle agree to the levying of a bounty — and, thus, the figurative fur flew.

As can be seen from this encounter, the red fox definitely has its admirers, though the creature's numbers have definitely declined since I first set foot in the Great South Woods. The advent of the coyote is indisputably the primary cause of this decline. Coyotes will kill foxes and their kits whenever the opportunity presents itself. They also kill and devour other wildlife that would otherwise be available to the fox as prey.

When I first arrived here, red fox tracks and signs could be seen on just about every logging road and trail in the woods of the region. I frequently caught a whiff of their scent. That obvious sign of yore is now no more. Red fox sign is now much more scattered and cryptic, reflecting in large measure the more furtive creature they have now become. No longer does the "red prince" prance with impunity in the moonlight.

This was borne out by recent surveys conducted by the Wildlife Conservation Society of Saranac Lake. In an effort to survey populations of Adirondack predators, the WCS installed a network of remote sensor cameras (a.k.a. "buck cameras") at suitable locations all throughout the Adirondack Park. The results of this survey confirmed that red foxes were, in large measure, restricted to the vicinity of roadsides and outlying houses in the Adirondack Park. This corroborated my observations, since I know several red fox dens in the vicinity of the hamlets of Star Lake and Cranberry Lake. The thinking of wildlife experts is that the red fox gains some measure of security there, since the coyote normally appears more loathe to inhabit these human-influenced areas. This measure of security is not infallible, however. Coyotes have been known to occasionally enter hamlets to pick off house cats, and they could easily extend this familiarity to the red fox.

Even in its current altered habitat, though, it is still nice to have the "prince of the moonlight" around. Who knows? If the wolf becomes a regular inhabitant of the Adirondacks, and coyote numbers inevitably decline, the red fox could once again re-establish itself in respectable numbers throughout the Great South Woods.

Gray Fox

Admittedly a "canine with a difference," the gray fox appears to be in the process of establishing himself in far greater numbers in the Adirondacks. Besides his un-canine ability to climb trees, the gray fox exhibits his difference by a preference for establishing his dens in rocky fissures and caves, as well as hollowed-out tree stumps — all in marked contrast to red foxes, coyotes, and wolves, which prefer to dig their dens in suitable soil. The snug security of the gray fox dens makes them far less susceptible to being dug out by marauding coyotes than is the case with the red fox's dens. For this reason, among others, it has been speculated that gray foxes are far more compatible with coyote populations than are red foxes. This appears to be the case in our are, and it seems likely to be at least partially responsible for the rapid rise in gray fox numbers at the seeming expense of the red fox.

Although I've only seen one gray fox in our area myself, evidence of their mounting numbers can be found all through the Adirondacks. A gray fox was killed by a motor vehicle right near the entrance to the Adirondack Park Agency Visitors Interpretive Center in Newcomb two years ago. These foxes have also exhibited a decided tendency to appear in the vicinity of outlying houses in hamlets. This tendency becomes even more marked in winter. Friends with houses in the hamlets of Star Lake, Long Lake, and Newcomb have all played host to family groups of gray foxes recently. A family of gray foxes that makes regular nocturnal forays has also consistently entertained Clarence Petty at his family homestead in Coreys.

I also have begun to see increasing numbers of gray fox tracks in the winter snows. Tracks are the only signs of this species that I can recognize with any degree of accuracy, as scat and other markings widely overlap with red fox.

A local trapper in Cranberry Lake recently caught his first gray fox in over two decades of trapping in this area. He at first wondered if it was one of the off varieties of red fox, so unfamiliar was he with the gray fox.

There is no doubt that gray fox numbers are increasing, perhaps dramatically, in the Great South Woods. There is also no doubt that this upsurge in numbers is actually, at least in historic terms, a re-colonization, as archaeological records show that gray foxes were widely distributed in our area several hundred years ago. Whether global climate change can account for their increasing numbers is something only the future will reveal.

Bobcat

There is little doubt that the bobcat, the most common feline in the Adirondack Park, is another species that has had its population levels negatively impacted by the Eastern coyote's colonization of the Adirondacks.

From the beginning of the 20th century until well into its second half, the bobcat reigned more or less as the supreme predator hereabouts.

Photo by Uta Wister

A bobcat takes a nap under a ledge.

They were seemingly everywhere. Fire tower observers, in a number of instances, broke the monotony of their solitary watch by taming young bobcats and raising them as pets. Young bobcats were also caught to supply zoos and circuses, as in the case at Streeter Lake which I mentioned in the first "Great South Woods" book.

Deer yards, in particular, seem to hold a special fascination for the medium-sized lynx. A trip to the vicinity of any of the larger Adirondack deer yards revealed abundant signs of bobcats and, not infrequently, a sighting of the cat itself. Local trappers who were particularly proficient could expect to harvest a half dozen or more bobcats, something unheard of today.

Suddenly, around 1960, things began to change. Bobcat numbers began to spiral downward, just as coyote populations began to increase dramatically. Most biologists and local woodsmen did not believe the two happenings were a coincidence. In fact, they were not.

Eastern coyotes impact bobcat populations on two levels. One is by direct predation, usually on the kittens of the bobcat. While a mature bobcat is more than a match for any coyote, Eastern or otherwise, the female bobcat has to leave her kittens in order to hunt. That is when the kittens are most vulnerable to being killed by coyotes.

The second level of impact is that coyotes generally out-compete bobcats in hunting more effectively, thus leaving the bobcats with a paucity of prey. Scientists call this "interference competition," and there is no doubt this has occurred here. The winter pack formation of the Eastern coyote probably confirmed this advantage to them at the expense of the bobcat.

A number of different groups in the Adirondacks used to hunt bobcats with dogs. I remember that, in the 1980s, there was the group from downstate who hunted the area around Massawepie Pond in what is now known as the Watson's East Wild Forest. As I recall, they had a fair success rate and seemed to enjoy running their hounds as much as harvesting a bobcat. They stopped coming sometime in the 1990s, and I know of no other group that has taken up the mantle since.

About a decade ago, however, my winter tracking forays began to reveal a change regarding the status of bobcats locally. Bobcat numbers, as disclosed by their tracks in the snow, began to mount a gradual, modest upsurge in numbers. This has continued to this day. Local trappers have also confirmed this observation to me. In November 2004, after a drought of almost two decades, I finally spotted my fourth bobcat in the wild — right in back of my house!

Bobcats have always been elusive and not easy to see. Even an accomplished senior woodsman like Clarence Petty has informed me that he has seen only eight in the wild. The sight of a bobcat in the wild is truly a special event. Still, the current increase, even if it happens to taper off, should give some fortunate people an increased opportunity to spy one of these glorious felines in their free and unfettered state.

Pine Marten

When we come to the presence of pine marten in the Great South Woods, we are presented with quite a different situation than that which applies to most other species. Since the marten is quite furtive and elusive in habit, it is much more difficult to document, or even to determine, any dramatic increase or decrease in population levels. This is compounded by the fact that currently there is no legal trapping season in our area.

Nevertheless, it is my instinctive feeling that there has been a pronounced increase in marten numbers in our area in the past three decades. I now see — and hear — more and more marten signs in quite varied areas of the Great South Woods. The Massawepie scout area, with its large hemlock and white pine, is especially productive when it comes to revealing signs of marten. The interior areas of the Five Ponds

Wilderness also appear to host good numbers of marten. Their presence here does not appear to be restricted to old-growth areas, although they might achieve their highest population levels in the ancient forests. DEC personnel quite recently came unexpectedly across abundant signs of marten near the cutover hardwoods of the Long Pond Easement lands in the town of Colton.

Photo courtesy Newcomb Visitors' Interpretive Center

A pretty pine marten visits the VIC.

As detailed in *The Great South Woods*, I first became aware of the martens in my own locale upon seeing one dead in a conifer trap. The marten was trapped inadvertently in a fisher set by John Simpson of Star Lake. John, a noted woodsman and friend who knew of my interest in the subject, showed me the carcass immediately before he went out and buried it. This would seem to indicate that the tenure of marten in this area does have some history, as it is now almost 30 years since this incident transpired. Still, from what I am observing by tracks and by listening, my instinct tells me that marten are in the process of making a slow, but steady, local population increase.

In accord with this, the local DEC Fish and Wildlife Division office in Watertown is conducting surveys in our area to determine the exact status of the marten here. Their hope is that this survey will determine if marten numbers are actually rising and if that increase is sufficient to warrant extending the open trapping season to our area from the Central Adirondacks, where it is currently in effect.

Personally, I remain dubious as to whether the population is now high enough to warrant an open season here. Still, the marten has enough of the furtive animal in him to possibly prove me wrong. Either way, the result of this survey should prove quite interesting.

Bald Eagle

Bald eagle populations in the Great South Woods have a pronounced difference from populations of most other species living in the area: Different populations of bald eagles inhabit the area in the summer and winter. Many of the summer eagles, which often are nesting pairs, move on by autumn. They are replaced by a different slate of individual eagles, which mainly migrate from the north.

Neither of these distinct population groups were in evidence when I arrived in the North Country in 1971.

Bald eagles were restored as a nesting species to the avian fauna of our area through a method called "hacking." In this process, baby eagles are removed from the nests in Alaska and planted in man-made "nests" in the area where they are to be reintroduced. This transfer of abodes requires great care so that the imprint of humans is kept to a minimum during feeding the young. Several of these hacking sites were immediately adjacent to our area in the 1980s.

Photo by Uta Wister

Our nation's symbol

Beginning in the 1990s, bald eagles began to nest as a regular occurrence. Returning year after year to the same nest locations, bald eagles have established known mating sites at Blake Reservoir, Sols Island on the Raquette River, Wolf Pond, and at Nehasane Lake. There are probably other nesting pairs whose locations have not been confirmed. Usually, but not always, the nesting pairs are successful in fledging at least one chick. The nests are usually located in a towering white pine, and eagles can often be observed patrolling the skies over the rivers and large lakes of the Great South Woods in a constant quest for fish to satisfy their appetite. Occasionally, they will steal a fish from a lesser raptor, the osprey, although I have been a witness to this pilfering only once locally.

With the advent of winter, an entirely different bald eagle scenario is played out in our area. Many of our local birds migrate and are replaced by eagles arriving from Canada. Since there is almost no open water here in the average winter, it is readily apparent that the eagles have had to resort to alternative food supplies in this period of want. They have done this by relying on a steady and ample supply of venison for sustenance in winter.

If anything, there are even more eagles present in winter. The most I have witnessed at one time were 20 bald eagles on a deer carcass in the town of Clare. I have heard of reliable reports of up to 30 birds feeding at deer carcasses at this site and at an alternate spot near Sevey's Corner, where the Department of Transportation disposes of road-killed carcasses. Both immature bald eagles and the snowy-headed adults are usually present, often sharing the carcass with a veritable horde of ravens. The ravens are quite wary of the eagles and readily make way for them. In fact the ravens, which appear to monitor the doings of the Eastern coyote prior to their making a kill, are often the first on the scene of a carcass, only to have their pride of place usurped by eagles.

The bald eagle is a truly noble and fitting national emblem, despite the misgivings of Benjamin Franklin, who preferred the wild turkey. It is also fitting that eagles, along with the moose, have made the most dramatic changes in population levels in the Great South Woods. Both species have progressed from the non-existent to the almost plentiful in a period of a few decades.

Other Raptors

The Great South Woods is singularly fortunate in still possessing a nearly complete slate of breeding raptors. With the possible exception of the golden eagle, all of the avian predators once present here are still around and, to greater or lesser degree, are still plying their deadly ways on their chosen prey species.

I have seen decided population changes in raptor numbers in the past three decades. Some of the changes have been nearly imperceptible, while others are quite pronounced. In the latter category, three species spring readily to mind. One of these has apparently colonized our area from elsewhere. A second has possibly done the same thing, although scattered populations may have been present initially. A third raptor species, on the other hand, has experienced a steep decline in population in our region.

The raptor that has apparently colonized our area is the merlin, a modest-sized falcon. Even here, there is the slight possibility that the bird was always present locally, albeit in decidedly lesser numbers. I vividly recall a number of sightings I had in the 1980s in the vicinity of Leonard Pond. I relayed these sightings to Mike Peterson, a noted Adirondack ornithologist; but his conclusion at the time was that these merlins were probably early autumn migrants. It is somewhat difficult now not to wonder what their exact status was at that time.

Nevertheless, merlins began to be seen and were confirmed to be breeding all over the Adirondacks by the mid-1990s. There was a minor explosion in numbers, with the first successful nestings being verified in the vicinity of the St. Regis Canoe Area and then spreading fairly rapidly to the edge of the High Peaks Wilderness. From there, it was only a matter of time until they expanded their range into the Great South Woods, which they proceeded to do around the turn of the 21st century.

A breeding pair was confirmed in the Cranberry Lake Campground, while others were noted throughout the summer in the town of Pitcairn. During the breeding season, I noted several birds around the Bog River Flow, although I was unable to discover any nest. I believe that a report of breeding was subsequently confirmed near this location.

Whether the previous undocumented status of the merlin here was due to a lack of local birders, rather than a lack of the birds themselves, is a moot question. They are now present, and they are definitely increasing in number.

Similar to the merlin's situation, I did not see any sign of the red-tailed hawk when I first arrived in the North Country in 1971. I was immediately struck by its absence because this large raptor was, at the time, common in most other rural areas of the state. Large trees for nesting and some moderate-sized open areas for hunting were all that seemingly were required for them to flourish.

Around 1980, however, I first began to note signs of red-tailed hawk during the summer. Many of the sightings were around large beaver flows, which had progressed to the point where they were approaching the final stage of becoming a meadow before reverting back to woodland. Hawks apparently find this a suitable substitute for the pastures of downstate and the St. Lawrence Valley. This presents us with an interesting situation, as these dry beaver flows were probably the original habitat of these raptors before the advent of man-made pastures. Also interesting is the fact that, unlike other areas, I often find their nests placed in conifers here, rather than the tops of large hardwoods. I personally know of one such nest in the Cranberry Lake Wild Forest that has been used for a number of successive years.

When we move on to the case of another pint-sized falcon, the population trend is quite different. American kestrel numbers have been declining statewide, and our region is no exception. Kestrel populations have decreased sharply in the Great South Woods; and I no longer see them nesting contentedly on electric wire as I frequently did when I arrived here. Populations began to spiral downward here beginning around 1990. By the end of that decade, kestrels were mostly vanished from the few pasturelands and cemeteries where they had previously plied their trade around the hamlet of Fine.

It is unclear at this time what catalyst has triggered this change in the kestrel's fortunes, either here or elsewhere in the state. As they are cavity nesters, it has been suggested that they are following in the footsteps of the bluebird a generation earlier. Whatever the cause, I hope that the trend can be reversed.

The raptor situation locally only serves to illustrate what has so often been proclaimed regarding wildlife: "in nature, the only constant is change."

Ravens

An especially poignant recollection I have from the early 1970s is scrambling around the wall cliff just below the summit of Cat Mountain on a raw April day. The object of my quest that day was to spy, with my own eyes, the nest of a raven that reposed on a ledge of that cliff. So scarce were ravens at the time that this nest was one of the very few known to exist anywhere in the Adirondack Park.

How the situation has turned around today! Ravens are ubiquitous throughout the Adirondacks and have actually extended their range dramatically. The St. Lawrence Valley, the Catskills, and even areas beyond now host this shining black corvid, which Edgar Allen Poe depicted as the personification of evil. Although several factors could be at play here in accounting for this population upswing, the main impetus appears to be the year-round presence of a coyote population in all areas of the park. Unlike crows, which often migrate to the St. Lawrence Valley in winter, ravens are restricted to their home range all year. The presence of Eastern coyotes on a regular basis now provides the ravens with a steady, dependable supply of leftover prey carcasses from which to scavenge all year round.

Ravens compete with turkey vultures in summer for access to carcasses, and perhaps also for nesting sites. Roadsides at the crack of dawn during this time of year occasionally provide the spectacle of these two scavengers doing a tandem dance with each other as they attempt to gain sole access to the carcasses lying flattened on the road from the night before. Ravens are indeed quite resourceful at securing food in summer, and I would wager they have a higher intelligence level than most avian species. I suspect the epithet "bird-brain" does not apply to ravens. I have seen them using and feeding on snakes, worms, berries, garbage, voles, eggs, and a plethora of other food in addition to carcasses. On one unhappy but memorable occasion, ravens methodically fed on every single sprout growing from six rows of corn I had planted, though the garden had been treated with a foul-smelling deterrent specifically intended to thwart them. The ravens waited until the smell had dissipated, by which time the sprouts were six inches tall, and then proceeded to remove every one of them from all six rows. Through my chagrin and annoyance, I began to see how people in the 19th century, like Edgar Allen Poe, perceived them as diabolical.

Turkey Vulture

Photos by Uta Wister

Ravens in winter haunt the vicinity of deer carcasses and are a perfect foil for the bald eagle in this endeavor. Ravens often alert the eagles to the presence of a carcass, only to have the eagles usurp their place at the carcass. In areas where more than one deer carcass is present, ravens and eagles may both be seen feeding in close proximity to each other, usually with an uneasy truce. At such times and places, I have seen up to 20 ravens feeding together simultaneously. Sevey's Corners, where the state DOT regularly deposits cervid road fatalities, is one area where this frequently occurs.

So prevalent are ravens today in the Great South Woods that I am hard pressed to recall what this forest was like when it was bereft of the hoarse croaks and aerial swoops of this impressive corvid.

WILD TURKEY

Ben Franklin's choice for our national emblem is perhaps the most prominent Adirondack wildlife species to display a classic dual personality. At times, it comes across as a member of the glorious game species: wily, wary and wild. At other times, its guilelessness seems to lend credence to the unflattering characterizations frequently used to describe it.

Whatever the true personality traits of this bird, wild turkeys in our area have undergone an explosive surge in population, which has taken them from the non-existent to the almost common. Wild turkeys are not only found on the periphery of the area but also maintain a presence near some of our most boreal areas, like Sabbatis, Wanakena, and Aldrich. This contradicts the prevailing wisdom of the 1970s, which proclaimed that wild turkeys would not survive in the Adirondacks because of the harsh winters. While the local winter is, indeed, a time of want for the wild turkey, enough of them do get through to ensure that the species passes on its DNA. Budding of local hardwood trees and grubs, which are scratched for in areas around springs and around vacated deer beds where snow has melted, usually ensures turkey survival locally.

The prevailing wisdom declares that the wild turkey populations in the Great South Woods stem from DEC releases in the nearby St. Lawrence Valley and on Fort Drum. However, there is an intriguing sidebar to this hypothesis that I find noteworthy. A number of local game clubs made unauthorized turkey releases from game-farm stock in this area in the 1970s. They stoutly proclaim today that the wild turkey presence locally stems from their endeavors. While this is certainly plausible, I do not consider it probable, if only because of the poor survival of farm-reared birds before the state began releasing only wild, trapped birds. It was only at this point that turkey populations started to soar — but we know only too well that nothing can be totally ruled out when dealing with a dynamic subject like wildlife.

In addition to weather, predation also serves as a check on local turkey populations. This is particularly true with regard to hens, which are especially vulnerable when brooding their eggs. From my observations, coyotes often take the females at this time, while raccoons often destroy the turkeys' eggs. Even male wild turkeys are occasionally preyed upon by great horned owls and bald eagles. Roosting in trees is a survival mechanism that wild turkeys have developed over the years.

While I admit I never imagined that I would see wild turkeys as common sightings when I first arrived here, I nonetheless consider them a welcome addition to the local fauna.

Other Wildlife Changes

There are a number of other wildlife forms whose populations have altered since my arrival in the North Country, and the status of these species has changed every bit as considerably as those just listed. I have decided to lump them together because of their generally small size, although their functions in any ecosystem are usually not insignificant.

The palm warbler, an arboreal bird of the bog lands, has gone from an unknown breeding status in our area to one where it can now be expected to be found breeding in fairly dense clusters in the several extensive peat lands for which the Great South Woods is renowned. The dramatically increased population of the palm warbler here is no longer in any doubt. What is in some doubt is whether this upsurge in numbers reflects an actual increase in population or whether it is merely a reflection of the previous paucity of bird watchers in our part of the Adirondack Park.

When we come to that striking nocturnal songster, the whippoorwill, there is no doubt that its steeply declined population is not due to any lack of human listeners. The simple truth is that its dramatic, three-part evening call simply does not resonate from the depth of the forest anywhere nearly as frequently as it did in the past. A perusal of my nature notes reveals that I heard one calling from the side of my house at 5 a.m. one day in May 2004, and that this was the first time I had heard its call in 15 years. This population decline appears to apply to most of its range in New York state. While a number of factors have been advanced to account for the whippoorwill's demise over a major portion of its range, there is of yet no definite consensus of what the main factor in this decline is.

There is no such ambiguity of cause when it comes to the decline of the Eastern wood peewee, a woodland warbler that has recently experienced a sharp decline of its numbers in the deciduous forests of our area. The decline here has been directly attributed to the destruction of the tropical Caribbean forests, where the peewee migrates in winter. Its plaintive breeding call formerly ranked with songs of the red-eye vireo and ovenbird as one of the defining sounds of our local hardwood forests in spring. This breeding call is almost never heard now around here. I vividly recall retired St. Lawrence University ornithologist, Ken Crowell, exhorting me fervently to listen intently for this call in my ramblings through forests of the southern part of St. Lawrence County. I did listen, frequently and intently, but rarely heard the call. My sadness at the virtual extinction of this call in our woods is perhaps rendered even more poignant by the irrefutable fact that the cause of this demise may be outside our ability to rectify, due to its origin in the Caribbean, where the forests of its winter range are being decimated — but who knows? Hope rises eternal, and remnants of those Caribbean forests might yet be saved through international efforts currently underway.

Finally, we come to an enigma: the perplexing status of the Canada goose in the North Country. Are any Canada geese truly wild now, or are they all just semi-feral? Most Canada geese in New York state are semi-feral at best, a pest to be hunted down. In the North Country, however, some geese live an existence under what approximates truly wild conditions. The Canada geese that were introduced to the large wildlife management areas of the St. Lawrence Valley, by dint of sheer numbers, can be said probably to lead at least a semi-wild existence. Those in the bays of Tupper Lake and Cranberry Lake lead a wild existence in spring and early summer, but then seem to deny it by grazing domestically on the grasses in front of the Ranger School and a municipal park in the village of Tupper Lake. In my opinion, the only truly wild Canada geese locally are the ones that try to eke out a living and raise their broods in isolated beaver ponds. The hitch here is that they often don't survive. The two I was keeping close tabs on — one in back of my house, the other in the town of Pierrepont — were both eliminated by coyote predation.

I guess all this shows that the status of local Canada geese populations presents us with a genuine puzzle. Only the passage of time will determine if any truly wild geese survive in the Great South Woods.

CONCLUSION

As becomes readily apparent from this litany, there have been tremendous shifts among wildlife populations in the past four decades. What lies ahead? If nothing else, this creates a royal incentive to stay healthy and remain around as long as possible to see what the future will bring.

7
FOREST POTPOURRI

INTRODUCTION

This chapter links together seven disparate topics that are close to my heart. Included are musings on a pair of trees of which I am deeply enamored. I delve into my winter love of snow tracking, expounding on the ecology of a blow-down as well as explaining elements of the wild around an old homestead. To round out the canopy of this forest potpourri, I've included discussions of some recent DEC acquisitions and their natural attributes, along with a discussion of some of the local flora and their usage by humans, both now and in past.

Ode to a Beech

Could a tree be found that is more pleasing than the beech, with its serene, light-grey sheen of bark lighting up the gloom of an autumn forest? Its bark is so pleasing that certain types of vandals find they are unable to restrain themselves from disfiguring it, usually with their initials.

The minor-sized mast that beech produces is itself so nutrient-packed that it is irresistible to a broad array of wild creatures spanning the spectrum of mammal and avian life. Deer, bears, raccoons, foxes, coyotes, fishers, and martens all relish this delicacy, as do the more conventional turkeys, grouses, squirrels and chipmunks. The nut of the beech provides sustenance to all of them. In years when beechnut production peaks, the forest abounds with these creatures, which utilize the extra energy provided by the nuts to heed the biblical admonition to increase and multiply. Conversely, when beechnut production is off, there is a decided paucity in the numbers of some of these creatures.

But was there ever an earthly paradise that remained forever undefiled? For the noble beech and the myriad creatures depending on it for sustenance, this defilement can come in the form of an alien insect, a species of aphid that probably hitched a ride to the United States on the imported European beech. This aphid established a beachhead early, and in a relatively short time it had spread to the Adirondacks, where it began to ravage mature native beech trees. The white, cottony froth that this "scale insect" exhibited when feeding on the bark of beech soon became a common sight in the forests of the Great South Woods. The insect did not kill the beech outright, but the many minute perforations it left on the bark from its feeding provided ingress for the spores of two forms of fungus that promptly proceeded to further devastate the tree by feeding on living tissue inside the bark. One of the fungi, the false tinder conk, is native; the other, the beech scale fungus, is an exotic species like the scale insect that initiated the destruction. Feeding of the fungus on the interior parts of the tree eventually culminates in the death of the tree, often by weakening it structurally and making it susceptible to wind blow, which topples the tree. The spores of the fungus can be observed as a reddish "stain" on the bark of the beech; when this is noticed, it is evidence that the disease is fairly well progressed and that the demise of the beech is imminent. Foresters refer to this complex cycle as beech scale disease. The initial killing front usually destroys most of the mature beeches in a stand, while the fungal spores that are still present threaten the remaining beeches at what appears to be even a younger age.

So what can the legions of Adirondack life forms that most depend on beeches expect? While taking a crystal ball to peer at the future is often iffy, I will hazard a guess that all the species concerned will remain in the Great South Woods, although some of them may have to persist at a lower population level. Beechnuts will still be present, albeit at a reduced level from the small-class trees still present in the stands.

An unusual situation occurs among trees that are close to succumbing to the disease. In a Darwinian effort to perpetuate their genes for posterity, the dying beeches produce an inordinately high number of beechnuts during their last few years of existence. While deer rarely browse the buds of beech, the beech thickets that ensue from the root sproutings of the dying beech have proven to be a bonanza to local snowshoe hare populations.

Still, a walk in a present-day beech grove quickly reveals that a number of things are not as they were before the advent of the beech scale complex.

I retain vivid memories of nature walks a decade or more ago, when I could count on encountering a large beech tree whose bark bore the imprint of bear claws left when the creature climbed the tree to harvest its succulent beech nuts. After this was pointed out to the participants in the hike, there was sure to be an avid discussion regarding both beech and bears. The climbing bears usually sat on a sturdy crotch high in the tree and proceeded to gather in all branches within reach so as to harvest the beech nuts on them; in doing so, they invariably left a jumbled bunch of disfigured branches. These jumbled branches stood out clearly in the leafless trees of winter and were referred to as "bears' nests." Today they are mostly a thing of the past, since there are now relatively few beech trees mature enough in stature to support climbing black bears.

Dead and dying beech trees harbor an interesting assortment of fungal brackets on their bark. Prominent here are two striking and common brackets, the artist conk and the tinder (or hoof) conk. Neither of these woody fungi are implicated in the demise of the beech, as they are primarily saprophytes that feed on dead wood, thereby eventually helping to recycle the trees. The true culprit here is the false tinder conk, the fruiting bracket of the Necteria fungus, which can be seen on the beech well after the tree's death. I often see a very special grayish lichen, large and oblong-shaped, that grows on the bark of the mature beech. I call it the "target lichen," because in an earlier era it served as an emergency sighting for a deer rifle. I see this "target" lichen growing nowhere else but on the beech, and I can't help but wonder what will happen to it when large beeches are totally eliminated from the forest.

Finally, I have to make mention of one other reputed aspect of the beech that has resonated at a somewhat personal level for me. This is the alleged tendency of the beech to exhibit the most pronounced resistance to lightning strikes of any tree in the Great South Woods. A venerable woodsman pointed this out to me when I first arrived in the Adirondacks, over three decades ago. Taking heed of this advice, I deliberately sought out a large beech in order to survive two of the most severe electrical storms I have ever encountered while being afoot in the forest. I do not know if the beech/lightning relationship is myth or fact — but, for what it's worth, I do know that I survived both storms. I now wonder what will replace these old, venerable beech trees in future electric storms.

Snow Tracking

Since my youth, I have been fascinated by the wanderings of the creatures of the wild. Who went where? Why did they go there? What

Photo courtesy Natural History Museum of the Adirondacks

Winter wildlife watching.

did they do when they arrived? All these questions and more can be answered by tracking them in the snows of winter.

Intimacy with the furtive wanderings of the creatures of the wild begins first with the identification of the species we are actually seeing. A good tracking guide will be indispensable here; but even so, there will be times of puzzlement and occasional frustration. This often results from the different forms that snow can take once it has landed on the ground.

Tracks can be on a snow surface that is icy, powdery, or even in the process of melting from the rays of the sun. Tracks that are icy or melting may become disfigured and distorted to the point where they are difficult to discern. Melting tracks, in particular, can be greatly enlarged beyond their original size. I find this often causes confusion as to identity, as such tracks may be mistaken for those of a similar but larger species. When the tracks in the snow are unclear, following the trail for a distance will usually reveal some diagnostic signs that will disclose the identity of the track maker. Patience and a little sleuthing ability are called for here; these can enhance the thrill of the "chase."

I have learned many facets of the habits and lifestyles of the secretive woodland creatures that are so loath to reveal their presence to us in person. I have attempted to share with others the knowledge I have acquired, and the pure joy of tracking itself, by leading numerous winter tracking forays over the past several decades. Some of these trips were sponsored under the auspices of the Adirondack Park Visitors Interpretive Center at Newcomb, the Indian Creek Nature Center, and the Adirondack Natural History Museum, whose permanent home is currently under construction in Tupper Lake. I hope I have been successful in these efforts.

Following is a summary of the more prominent mammal species of the Great South Woods, together with some of the knowledge I have gleaned from faithfully following their tracks through the snows of winter.

Snowshoe Hare

While the phrase "mad as a March hare" was coined mainly in response to the mating antics of the European hare in March, our native snowshoe hare can also be pretty frolicsome during the period of his annual mating, which starts in late March and extends through April. Their mating here is somewhat later than in Europe, a response to our longer winters; but when mating season finally comes to the Adirondacks, all its frantic activity is reflected by tracks in the snow. In fact, hare tracks are definitely more consistent in the mating season than they are earlier in the winter.

One surprising fact I have learned from tracking hares during the winter is that they can lie up for what appears to be an inordinate amount of time. Quite frequently, I will see no signs or tracks of hares in an area for three or four days when, quite suddenly, hare tracks miraculously seem to be all over the area, as if the animals had sprung up from the underlying bedrock. The only thing I can positively deduce from this is that hares are masters at the art of concealment and must deftly hide themselves under low-lying conifers, in blow-downs, and among the rocks of talus slopes. All this is revealed by tracks in the winter snow. How they survive without feeding during this time, I don't know, although hares are capable of feeding on the scat they have voided, and this may be a factor in enabling them to survive without otherwise feeding in the time of winter want.

An interesting tidbit in conjunction with the lying up of hares is that during this period, every bobcat and fisher in the area will search very precisely, from place to place, examining every spot where hares are likely to be concealed. Tracks in the snow disclose these paths of the predators, revealing that they have a special penchant for visiting every low-lying conifer for miles around.

Snowshoe hares are the base of the food chain in the Great South

Woods, and their wanderings, as shown by their readily recognizable tracks, have the potential to brighten what would otherwise be a drab winter day.

Fisher

Fisher tracks were once an Adirondack specialty, but now they may be sighted throughout the entire North Country, extending even into the Catskill region, where they occur as a result of translocation from this area. As mentioned in the account on hares, fishers investigate low-lying conifers as well as any other nook or cranny they may find as part of an intensive search for prey over their range. This thorough searching of habitat is reflected in the pattern of fisher tracks in the snow. The pattern is obvious in the constant crossing and re-crossing of tracks along a hiking trail as the fisher meanders back and forth along his route in a never-ending quest for prey.

It has been alleged that fishers hunt over a definite range and will visit each part of that range over a period of several days. While I believe this to be generally true, I do not believe such timing is always inevitable. For instance, fishers will stay put for an indefinite period of time around a concentrated food resource, such as carrion.

I have often found fishers walking on or alongside the paths that porcupines make as they plod through the snow. In this instance, the fishers appear to be hunting prey by specifically following the quarry, rather than by randomly searching the landscape. Silhouettes in the snow have shown me that fishers dispatch porcupines, both on the ground near their dens and high in the trees, where the porcupines feed on buds in winter.

Two other quirks of fishers that I have noticed over years of tracking are a tendency to avoid getting their feet wet and a decided preference for their own company. The former quirk is revealed by observations of fishers crossing over a narrow stream on the shaky branches of alders in order to avoid touching the shallow water. The other quirk is attested to by the fact that fisher tracks are invariably solo until the advent of March, their breeding season, when the large tracks of the male fishers and the considerably smaller ones of the female appear everywhere in tandem. This situation lasts for a week or so; then the two part, each proceeding again along their own paths. By then, the calendar is cresting April, and the snow cover is quickly receding.

I find fisher tracks of all stripes to be much more rare earlier in the snow season than later on. I do not know how to account for this, unless it relates to their high metabolic rate and an increasing need for energy food as the temperature drops.

This high metabolic rate probably also accounts for the fisher's hunting for prey around the clock during winter. This is certainly a bonus after a night of continual snow, when the only tracks that can be seen the next day are frequently those of fishers and weasels. Weasels have the same high metabolic rate in winter as fishers, a pertinent factor in their diurnal ramblings through the snow.

Whatever the reason, it is a pleasant surprise, and one that has saved me from some embarrassment on at least two occasions while leading snow tracking hikes at the Adirondack Park Visitors Interpretive Center.

Coyotes and other Canids

Four different canines may reasonably be expected to leave their tracks in the snows of an Adirondack winter, with the added perk of possibly finding a fifth. The size of the individual tracks now becomes critical in identifying the canid making them, along with the length of the stride and the width of the straddle. For a beginner, a good tracking guide will be indispensable in starting to learn to follow the activities of these nocturnal creatures by observing their tracks in the snow. I have personally found *Tracking and the Art of Seeing*, by Paul Rezendes, to be far and away the tops in the field.

Easily surpassing all other canine tracks in winter frequency are those of the Eastern coyote. Indeed, coyote tracks are probably the most common large-animal tracks seen in snow, as deer are usually localized in their winter concentration areas (yards) at this season. A short jaunt along any representative patch of Adirondack wild land will invariably cross the path of this relative newcomer to the area.

Coyotes are usually in a pack at this time of year to better facilitate the hunting of the white-tail deer. The maximum number of coyotes I've seen in a pack is eight. Despite this, I occasionally see reflected in the snow that coyote packs are primarily hunting snowshoe hare, even in the midst of extensive deer yards such as Sevey's Corner, where deer are practically behind every tree. Coyotes are not the apex predators that wolves are. I also see frequent evidence of solo or paired coyotes where they have plunged into thick conifer thickets, much as bobcats do, in order to flush out hares.

Coyotes regularly move along trails and old jeep roads, marking them as their territory with their scat and urine. Coyotes often walk along each side of a trail, off in the woods, in order to outflank prey and drive it to the members of the pack that are walking on the path. I believe they systematically hunt in this fashion for both deer and hare, as signs of this activity are quite frequently observed in winter. The snows also disclose where coyotes have scratched in the snow, similar to a domestic dog's markings. I feel this is also a form of communication, since I've observed scratching not only along trails but also at the site of kills and carrion, where scratching exists with scat, as it does on the trail.

Other tidbits that I have discerned from winter tracking include the fact that coyotes commonly walk exactly in each other's tracks, especially in deep snow — more proof of this bonding. The maximum jump I have noticed that they make is eight feet or so. They jump as they are running, chasing prey; but I also have noticed they often will run when passing in sight of a house, only to resume their normal gait once they have entered the woods.

There are other, larger canids whose tracks I occasionally see in the snowy Adirondack woods of winter. These tracks conform to the general outline of the coyote's in shape, except that they are between four and five inches in total length. I usually see these tracks in several places during an average winter. The current year (March 2005) is the only winter so far when I have not come upon them. These tracks belong to the "Eastern" or "Canadian" wolf, which has just been recognized as a separate species from the gray wolf, based on DNA analysis. Almost invariably, when I notice the tracks, they appear to be segregated from typical coyote tracks. Indeed, on two distinct occasions, I have seen where coyotes, when coming on these large tracks, have deliberately veered off their course. Once, three coyotes stopped at the line of larger tracks and actually retraced their paths exactly along the path from which they had just come. My snow tracking has never revealed a full pack of these animals, but I have often seen them paired.

The tracks of the still-larger gray wolf are similar to the outline of a large domestic dog, in distinct contrast to the Eastern wolf, whose track outline is simply like that of a huge coyote. While I have occasionally seen tracks similar to those of the gray wolf in the Great South Woods, I have not been able to identify them with any degree of certainty since I was, in every instance, unable to completely rule out the possibility that the tracks in question could have been made by "man's best friend."

There are, of course, smaller canines whose tracks are also reflected in the snows of winter. One of them, the red fox, has been present forever in the Adirondacks, or at least since the receding of the last of the glacial ice. The other, the gray fox, was formerly only present on the periphery of the Great South Woods but has recently extended its range throughout the entire Adirondack Park.

Red fox populations have declined dramatically of late, apparently in response to the advent of the Eastern coyote upon the local scene. Their tracks are no longer ubiquitous along area trails and Jeep roads, where they long ruled. These paths now mirror the tracks of the Eastern coyote as they go along their route, almost to the complete exclusion of red fox sign. Red foxes are still present, but it is obvious they are now much more furtive in their daily doings, the better to go undetected by coyotes. There is evidence that their numbers are now concentrated on the outskirts of hamlets and in the vicinity of isolated homesteads on the forest edges. I now find their dens far more often in these locations, where coyotes are usually somewhat more loath to go.

Red fox tracks differ from coyotes' in being solo from early winter until the latter part of February, when I begin to see them paired in preparation for the spring breeding season. The young are born in an April den that is often still surrounded by snow. It is nice that the red fox is still present in the Adirondacks, but I have to admit that I miss the odor of his musk, which was so liberally deposited along area paths in days of yore.

The newcomer, the gray fox, has tracks that are somewhat smaller and rounder than the red fox's, and laid with a shorter stride. They stay closer together as family units than do red foxes during winter, as groups of three and four individuals have been seen together feeding in or near the hamlets of Star Lake and Tupper Lake in January. I have seen gray foxes following the slides of otter and the troughs of porcupines for a considerable distance through the winter snows. While this obvious dislike of snow depths puts them at a disadvantage in the Great South Woods, they do have one decided advantage going for them in our area. Their dens are mainly in rock ledges and fissures, along with hollow logs that barely encompass their bodies, thus making the kits of gray fox less susceptible to predation by the larger-bodied coyotes than the kits of the red fox, which usually reside in the open in dug dens. Gray fox thus appear to be better able to coexist with coyotes and may also have prospered with the decline of red fox populations.

Bobcats and Other Felines

Feline tracks in the snow differ in a number of important aspects from canine tracks. For starters, all wild Adirondack felines are invariably solitary at this time of year, in contrast to some canines, as well as being far scarcer on the landscape than their fellow carnivores. In addition, I have noticed that cats generally are far more deliberate and meticulous in their hunting habits; and this fact is usually conveyed in their tracks. Still, bobcat and coyote tracks may occasionally be confused with each other, particularly when solitary coyotes are hunting hares or when coyotes in a pack have one of the members present in the peripheral flank and removed from the other members of the pack. In such instances, I usually have to follow the tracks for a distance. Eventually, bobcats will do something that unmistakably distinguishes them from coyotes, like walking deliberately on downed logs or digging a hole in the snow to void their scat. Then, too, the bobcat may spring up on to a glacial erratic simply for the pure joy of gazing out into the forest.

One interesting piece of knowledge I have gleaned from several decades of snow tracking is that bobcat tracks are far more common early in the winter, in the snows of November and December. This has proved true without exception for the 22 years during which I have been keeping records of such things. I must admit to being puzzled as to why this should be so. One possible contributing factor could be the migration of bobcats, along with deer, to the deer's winter concentration areas, where there are so many deer tracks that other tracks are not easily deciphered. Another possibility is that younger, smaller bobcats might succumb to starvation later in the winter, especially if they are unable to make a deer kill. Several recent studies have suggested that this theory may be factual in cold, snowy areas like the Adirondacks, where most small prey is protected by the snow pack. Bobcat tracks, though, have been definitely increasing for the past decade, as the animals apparently adjust to the presence of coyotes, as explained in another chapter.

Not all feline tracks in winter are bobcat. While the overwhelmingly majority of them are, I have on nine occasions over a quarter century witnessed tracks made by cougar and Canada lynx, the "creatures of the shadow." As in the case of the canine, a good field guide is indispensable in distinguishing between these different tracks, with the size of the tracks being only one of the criteria used.

I have seen cougar tracks five times, the long tail of the cat leaving a drag on two of them. On another occasion, a cougar left a thirty-one-inch stride between tracks on a clean two inches of late-March snow. Amazingly, out of the several score of tracks left by the cat, two of them distinctly registered five toes, with none of the tracks showing claws, as is the propensity of cats. In addition to the 23-foot jumps on a pond that a cougar made, an account of which I gave in the first "Great South Woods" book, I have also seen signs in snow of where a cougar headed straight down what appeared to be an almost perpendicular 20-foot cliff. Only a feline! Four of the five cougar tracks I trailed meandered about the landscape in the way of a bobcat. The one track that followed a more or less straight trajectory was that of an apparent female with a kitten.

While on three occasions in summer I have noticed where cougars had raked leaves up into a small mound along their path, I have not observed them indulging in this activity of leaving an identifying "scrape" in the snows of winter.

Because of its adaptation to snow conditions, the Canada lynx may leave a trail as a large as that of a cougar; although a large male lynx will weigh 40 pounds to a cougar's 150. This large foot size of the lynx is mainly a response to the snowy conditions in which they usually reside. Two of the lynx tracks I have seen had a very short stride, and all four of my sightings of lynx tracks showed where the lynx had barely broken through the crust of the snow. This is in stark contrast to where the cougar tracks sank much deeper into the snow. The hairs on the soles of the lynx's feet, plus the lighter body weight compared to cougar, account for the condition of the snow tracks of these two splendid predators. On one occasion, I saw the tracks of both a Canada lynx and a bobcat hunting hares in Peavine Swamp, near Wanakena. This was a special day, to be treasured and long remembered, as indeed is any day when I spy the tracks of one of these two wondrous felines.

Other Tracks

The otter and the mink are two aquatic members of the weasel tribe whose numbers, as disclosed by tracks in the winter snow, do not seem to fluctuate from year to year, as is so often the case with other predators. Winter after winter, their tracks appear to vary only minimally in abundance.

Bounding fisher

Photos courtesy Newcomb Visitors' Interpretive Center

The otter is famous for his slides, usually depicted as going down slopes into water. Actually, otters in winter quite frequently slide on a level surface; and I've followed some of these slides a considerable distance in the snow. The otter, in addition to the slide, also employs the 2-by-2 bound and 3-by-4 lope of the fisher.

When using this mode of travel, the tracks of the otter may at first be confused with those of the fisher, until the outline of the otter's thick tail is shown. How the otter does travel in winter! I once followed one from the icy waters of Star Lake up over the very crest of Maple Mountain, then on down to the Little River, all the way alternating between sliding and bounding.

There are two prominent members of the Adirondack fauna whose tracks in winter are most notable by their absence. The black bear hibernates the winter away, but his tracks may be seen in November and early December before he hides himself for his annual snooze. Adult males are the last to hibernate, and lately I have been seeing more of their tracks all through the recent relatively mild Decembers. On January 1, 2005, I saw the tracks of two different bears near Sabattis.

The tracks of beaver are similarly scarce in winter, as the beaver at this time is securely snug in his lodge with his hardwood food supply firmly ensconced in the mud under the cover of ice. This food supply dwindles all through the season and ultimately disappears as it is entirely consumed. Occasionally, this occurs in late February, and certainly by March. Now, an interesting and unusually shaped track may be seen in the snow as beavers exit the water to start cutting saplings to replenish their food supplies. The tracking path they leave as they transport the trees back to the water is now so intense that at first glance it appears a snowmobile was driven into the water. Pointing out this activity to participants of our March walks at the Adirondack Park Visitors Interpretive Center at Newcomb frequently enlivens the conversation. How the beaver can cut the understory trees at this time, something I don't begrudge them at all, except when they ascend a ridge to cut down beeches! Considering the problem beeches currently have in our forests, I admit to feeling a little poorly at this state of affairs.

Deer mice and short-tail shrews, both of whose tracks may be seen lacing the winter woods like those of so many fairy sprites, represent the tiny among woodland creatures. The smaller species of shrew and all the species of voles appear to stay safe and snug under the snow pack. I rarely see their tracks in the winter. I do, however, often see the tracks of both species of weasels as they tunnel into the snow banks in pursuit of these woodland waifs, a vivid reminder that in the balance of the ecosystem of the Great South Woods, there is no such thing as a state of guaranteed safety.

Ode to a Sugar Maple

The sugar maple, official tree of the state of New York, is a tree that produces such a golden sweetness that it would be pleasing to the palates of the angels. Could there be a nobler tree? I confess to a bias here, commencing with the first year I arrived in the Adirondacks. That year, I helped Lloyd Fenton in his sugar bush near Fine and was hooked for life on sugar maples. I also remember being somewhat more than slightly perturbed upon learning that a wholesaler from Vermont, who subsequently marketed all of that syrup as "pure Vermont maple syrup," picked up Lloyd's maple syrup.

Unlike beech, the leaves of young sugar maples are quite palatable to deer. If the numbers of feeding deer are high, they can prevent maple regeneration by completely eliminating seedlings from the forest understory. I have seen this in several places in the Adirondacks, always on large, private "parks" with a high deer population. Porcupines, too, relish the leaves of sugar maples, and they can often be seen in spring sitting high in the trees, feeding on the leaves. The relatively high calcium content of sugar maple leaves is the main reason for this love affair of porcupines and maples, and spring is the season of preference because the newly unfurled and emerging leaves have less toxic protection embedded in them than do the same leaves later on in the year. I have a private hunch that these leaves, being more "fresh," are more succulent and therefore more pleasing to the taste.

The calcium in the leaves of sugar maples eventually finds its way into the soil, thereby enriching it considerably. Indeed, with the exception of the relatively more rare white ash and basswood, the soil surrounding sugar maples is far richer in nutrients and less acidic than the soil under any other Adirondack tree. Because of this enrichment, I go to a sugar maple grove to look for that luxurious floral display that carpets the forest floor in spring before the unfurling of the canopy of leaves. Spring beauty, adder's tongue, wake robin, bellwort, as well as the occasional squirrel corn, Dutchman's breeches, white trillium, and hepatica are all present, jewels of joy, not only to the eye but also to the tongue that pronounces them. Blue cohosh and wild leeks are here, too, but they are often overlooked because they lack the brilliance of the other blooms just mentioned.

Invariably, there are hordes of wild native bees in up to a dozen species buzzing frantically close to the ground in a heroic effort to ensure that all these spring jewels are pollinated and will pass on their genes to their progeny. I frequently see a native "white" butterfly (as opposed to the alien cabbage white) here, trying to assist the bees in their efforts. There is, however, a tenet of nature that proclaims there is an exception for every rule. So, too, it is in pollination. While most of the flowers of the forest floor have this service performed by jeweled insects, the wake robin's pollination service is performed by drably attired flesh flies, undoubtedly attracted to the flower by the odor of carrion emanating from the plant.

While on the subject of insects, another invertebrate, the thrips, has been causing problems recently by their feeding on the trees. This is taking place mostly in New England. I have not observed it causing much of a problem in the Great South Woods, at least so far. The big potential problem for the beloved local trees will be the projected advent of global warming.

Flora and People in the Great South Woods

The Great South Woods can be compared to a natural garden, probably placed upon the landscape for a variety of reasons. Prominent among these reasons would certainly be a desire on the part of the Creator to assist mankind and make living more pleasant for our species. This has been the situation locally, probably beginning with the big-

Amanita-Death Angel

Photo by Jean McCormick

game hunters who showed up shortly after the last glaciers had receded, extending through the woodland Indians, and right down to the first Europeans arriving on the scene. It continues today, albeit in a reduced fashion, as people have become more removed from the natural scene.

When I first arrived in the Great South Woods in 1971, there was a considerably more lively interaction between local residents and species of local flora. Usually, but not always, this entailed harvesting parts of the plants as food of some sort. Various berries of different kinds were eagerly harvested by far more individuals than is the case today. I have fond memories reaching back to 1974 of seeming hordes of people parking in my driveway and proceeding about a half mile to a bare, rocky ledge on timber company land locally known as Pine Hill to gather blueberries to their heart's delight. No one ever seemed to come back with less than a bushel full of the succulent berries. Alas, this pleasant happening has not been played out on the local landscape for over two decades, and it is now beginning to fade from the memory of most concerned. While this may be partly attributable to the natural forest succession shading out some of the blueberries, I also feel that the culture of the high-tech age is playing a role in the current disdain toward old "woodsy" customs.

The very earliest berry that ripens for our pleasure is the shadberry, or June berry, which I find to be the sweetest of all. The problem is the difficulty in procuring enough of them to be satisfying, since they also are a fascinating attraction for black bears and songbirds, which invariably seem to pre-empt the treasures of this small tree for themselves. A common sight in the forest understory is the evidence of where black bears have pushed over the trees in securing the fruits. The trees often remain bent, and sometimes one may also notice a "witch's broom" created by the deformed slender branches of the shadberry, a result of the bear pulling the berries from twig to mouth. Keep a keen eye out for the signs, and you will gradually realize it is not an uncommon sight in our woods.

Red raspberries and blackberries are next to ripen, in that order. There is competition for these fruits also, since both black bears and raccoons find them irresistible. Chipmunks and ruffed grouse also relish them, and I've seen evidence of fox and coyotes having eaten them, also. Unlike shadberry, though, there always seems to be enough for all, including the diminishing numbers of fervent elderly people who still harvest them today.

The last fruit to ripen is that of the black cherry, which is probably the most beloved of all by wildlife. Humans, however, do not love the black cherry with equal fervor, for a number of reasons, one of which is that black cherries are usually found high up in the tree. The pit inside the fruit could also be a deterrent, as well as the fruit's resemblance to the chokecherry, which generally grows within easy reach but is aptly named. Anyone who avails himself of this bounty will soon discover they will not be going back for seconds. I sometimes glean cherry fruit from the forest floor and generally find it quite sweet. I must admit, however, that on a few occasions I was left wondering if I hadn't tasted chokecherry.

There are two other berries that are generally too harsh to the taste when eaten raw but which, when combined with other ingredients, can morph into a pleasant culinary experience. The high-bush cranberry, a wild viburnum, is one of these. Although quite sour when plucked from the branch, it evolves into a tasty morsel when incorporated in a pie with a liberal addition of sugar. Edna Sykes, the wife of John, from whom I purchased my house in 1973, regularly made these pies from the high-bush cranberries that grew in the cedar swamp behind their house.

Common elderberry, whose white blossoms enliven beaver dams, also has a berry that is quite sour to the individual taste, but its juice makes a beverage fit for the mythical gods when fermented into wine. Mary Hlad, an elderly Russian neighbor of mine, first made me aware of this when she annually left on the steps of my rustic camp the product of the berries she had picked from the swamps of my sprawling acreage on Tug Hill. Mrs. Hlad, a woman of temperance, always referred to this product as elderberry juice. Juice or wine, no matter what the name, I still savor the taste after all these years.

Wild currants of several species also grow locally. Apparently the fruit was utilized for jams in the 19th Century, but I haven't heard of anyone using them recently.

Two more members of the North Country flora that are harvested for food are cowslips and wild leeks. The leaves of cowslip plants make excellent "spinach," if they are harvested before the bright yellow blossoms appear. I was introduced to the goodness of cowslips as a salad shortly after my arrival in the North Country, and I ate them avidly in camp each spring. I still do.

I was similarly introduced to the joys of wild leeks early on when a good friend, Brent Kerr of Oswegatchie, showed me the way to prepare them. We had enjoyable times digging the onion-like bulbs right after the leaves on the forest floor put in an appearance, but an even more enjoyable time eating them.

There is one other plant that is not used for food but is accorded its weight in gold as both an aphrodisiac and a medicinal plant in Asia. Ginseng is its name, and its residence was scattered liberally through the rich northern hardwood forests of the Great South Woods. It still grows in those nutrient-enriched forest soils that also harbor the delightful spring vernal wildflowers. At one time, the area around Degrasse and Irish Hill Road in the town of Fine were noted for the many families engaged in the picking of ginseng for later transport to New York City or Asia. Because of the intensive harvesting, there has been a steep decline in numbers of ginseng plants, but it is still present, if you know where to look.

I learned this about a decade ago in St. Lawrence County, which is fortunate enough to have two of the most competent botanists in New York state as residents, Nancy Eldbloom and Anne Johnson. While participating in a floral survey of the county, these two were preparing to go to a site near Depeyster, which purportedly harbored a number of rare species of plants, including ginseng. The owner of the parcel in question was a Vietnam veteran who was alleged to be irascible at times. Nancy and Anne asked me to go along, just in case; and I promptly accepted. As it turned out, my presence was superfluous, as the owner of the land turned out to be quite an affable individual and host. Nonetheless, I was very grateful to be asked along, since it turned out to be a gorgeous and memorable day, during the course of which we discovered wild ginseng and several other rare plants that had previously been unknown to me.

Perhaps the final chapter in the interplay between people and plants in the Great South Woods is one that has yet to be written. Panax, or false ginseng, is a low herb that is fairly common in forests less rich in nutrients than those where ginseng thrives. I see it regularly in the Five Ponds Wilderness Area. Recently, the makers of decaffeinated green tea have been using panax as an ingredient in the composition of their health-conscious green tea product. They market it as "panax ginseng." Could this be a harbinger of a new era when people begin to scour the woods once again for the bounty it may provide? Time will tell.

Blow-Down Update

On July 15, 1995, a high-intensity windstorm descended on the Great South Woods, bringing in its wake massive destruction over a wide area. The storm, called a microburst, swept away everything in its path. Tens of thousands of acres of trees were leveled in the Five Ponds Wilderness Area of the Forest Preserve and in what is now known as the Whitney Wilderness. This singular event radically altered the forest landscape in a most dramatic fashion, changing its ecological processes and resulting in a general replacement of whole elements of fauna with quite different elements.

With the passage of a full decade, these changes are starting to become obvious. Ecologists predicted most of these changes, but there have been some surprises, too. I have seen these changes unfolding as I have led nature walks through the blow-down areas in Wanakena almost from the beginning. It has now become apparent that a few of the forecasts I made in my first *Great South Woods* book predicting ecological changes have not come to fruition. I don't stand alone though, since these predictions that failed to materialize had been echoed throughout the scientific community.

Most prominent among them was that the blow-down was going to precipitate an explosion in the white-tail deer population locally. This most definitely has not occurred. In fact, deer populations have experienced a modest decline in the area of the blow-down. While some anthropological factors — mainly involving DEC statutes — might be involved here, there is no doubt that the main impetus for the dwindled populations is the blow-down. The blow-down near Wanakena spans thousands of acres of fallen timber, all jumbled in every conceivable angle and direction to form an impenetrable maze for humans and an uncomfortable habitat for deer. It is evident now that deer mainly avoid the entire area, due to the awkwardness of movement through the tangled terrain and their increased vulnerability to predators while struggling to get through it. On numerous occasions, I have followed deer tracks for three-quarters of a mile on the hiking trail that bisects the blow-down. Time after time, they continue straight on the trail, without deviating in the slightest to enter the blow-down. This action is very atypical of deer; I can count on the fingers of one hand the times when I have seen this action duplicated in the thousands of miles of trail tramping I accumulated while researching the Adirondack trail guide I co-authored.

The sight of a doe romping practically unhindered through the blow-down is part of what misled me initially, validating the old axiom that natural processes should be observed on a sustained and continuous basis before a truism is pronounced. The blow-down has, in fact, removed significant local habitat for white-tail deer, resulting in an overall decrease in their numbers. The only partial compensation for this is that the impenetrability of the impacted area has resulted in a lack of hunter access, which translates into a reduced deer kill by hunters — good from the perspective of the deer, but not the hunter.

In contrast to deer, the blow-down has proved to be a positive thing for the snowshoe hare and has generally produced an increase in their numbers. This is more or less in conformance to what was expected. The increased complexity furnished by the fallen trees has provided enough cover to make the area begin to resemble the conifer cover that is the hare's preference. This has led the hares to occupy this habitat, from which they were formerly excluded when it was open hardwoods before the blow-down. However, they still find themselves susceptible to avian predators here, and this vulnerability ensures that the hare population in the blow-down is considerably less than in their preferred conifer thickets. Still, the upward surge in hare numbers here means an increase in the amount of prey and nutrients available to predators throughout the ecosystem. Black bear and bobcat numbers have exploded in the area as a direct result of the blow-down. While this was predicted, I must admit to being surprised by the sheer size of the increase for both species.

The reported bear harvest has exhibited a marked increase, probably as a result of the increased soft mast now produced mainly in the form of blackberries and raspberries. Some shadberries and chokecherries are also present now where before they, too, were absent from the closed forest. This mast is vital for fattening up the bears for all-important hibernating periods. This hibernating state has, in addition, been enhanced considerably by the large depressions under tip-up mounds created by the storm.

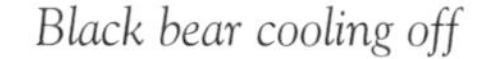

Black bear cooling off

Photo by Uta Wister

These have created ideal hibernating sites and undoubtedly increased the carrying capacity of black bears in the ecosystem.

Bobcat populations have also taken a sharp upsurge in response to the blow-down. Here it is the security and impenetrability furnished by the blow-down that has provided an ideal area for the female bobcat to den and raise her kits in security. Tracks, sometimes of paired individuals, are often seen going into the blow-down, especially at breeding time. Bobcats are now even seen on the roads of the hamlets by local residents, something that was unheard of before. The increased supply of hares has probably also furnished fuel for their increasing numbers.

When we come to the matter of bird populations, we enter a realm where there has been a replacement of one avian fauna for another complete and distinct bird fauna. The birds of thickets and semi-open areas have instantly supplanted the feathered creatures of a closed hardwood forest. White-throat sparrows and chestnut-sided warblers now sing, where once the ovenbird and red-eye vireo held sway from the canopy. The black-throated blue warbler, rose-breasted grosbeak, and scarlet are also, alas, no more. In their place, the common yellowthroat and song sparrow now proclaim their existence.

Woodpeckers have shown an overall increase, despite the fact that most of their feeding material now lies flat. This not only includes the prosaic hairy and downy woodpeckers but also a boreal specialty, the black-backed woodpecker. This latter species has thrived in response to the fair number of dead spruce that are scattered among the dead hardwood logs and stumps. The blow-down has, in fact, proven to be a bonanza to all species of woodpeckers, including the ant-eating flicker that thrives along the open path. One woodpecker that now appears to be missing is the large pileated woodpecker, which I often spied in the area when doing field work in the early eighties for the original *Atlas of Breeding Birds in New York State*, edited by Robert F. Andrle and Janet R. Carroll. The pileated woodpecker thrives on black carpenter ants, so perhaps these ants are not as common in the dead and downed timber now present as are bark beetles, whose populations have exploded with all the dead wood now available.

Change is inevitable when dealing with dynamic, living ecosystems. What is so extraordinary about the change at the blow-down sites is the magnitude of the change that has occurred in such a miniscule period of time.

Wildlife and Changes Around a Homestead

It has become evident over the years that certain wildlife species have become quite comfortable around the vicinity of rural homesteads. They have been attracted to these environs by the habitats created and by the food and shelter that have been inadvertently provided by man's alterations of the landscape in creating his domiciles. This is a brief account of one of those rural homesteads and the wildlife associated with it, along with the story of some wildlife changes that have transpired as one habitat has graded into another. The homestead in question is my own humble abode, and the wildlife observation begins with my purchase of the house in 1973.

Of all wildlife, it is the avian tribe that has been most effected by habitat change around my house. This change has come about mainly from the transformation of the open fields that once existed behind and on either side of the house, which have metamorphosed into young forests. The process of natural progression resulted in replacement of the field with hardwood forest, while a conifer forest arose upon an ill-advised planting of eight acres with red pine in 1974.

The alteration of the local avian life commenced within a few years. First to disappear were the meadowlark and the bluebird; even the construction of bluebird houses could not counteract the waning of their habitat. I witnessed an interesting aerial encounter between a bluebird and a tree swallow for possession of one of the nesting boxes one day in the late 1970s. I vividly recall the intensity of the encounter, but I can't seem to remember which species ultimately prevailed.

Field sparrows were next to go, although lately I have heard one across the road from my house, where the land was a hayfield for a decade longer than my land. This land is now growing back to scattered gray birch and cherry, so I was not terribly surprised to hear the enchanting, haunting twilight call of the woodcock there in early spring this year.

Next to wither away was the house wren, despite its having a handy nesting abode in the bluebird boxes I put up. I keenly miss the incessant rolling babble made on a bright June day by the male wren serenading his female, who remained safely ensconced with her young in the nesting box.

The phoebes that built their nest on a ledge of the front porch also departed eventually, although this could also be from mortality on their wintering grounds since the same phoebes return each spring to their previous nesting sites. Last year, I again heard the phoebes giving their charming identifying calls, but I was unable to find a nest.

The cedar waxwings, which nested in the large ornamental blue spruce behind the house, were also last seen about a decade ago, no doubt victims of the fields having reverted to forests.

One bird that has increased around the house is the robin. I wait in anticipation each year for its vocal heralding of another spring. I also wonder how robins manage to survive, as I continually find the ruins of their largish blue eggs scattered on the ground, victims of some successful predator. I imagine the multiple broods they produce each year enable them to withstand this constant assault.

Spring migration brings the myrtle warbler and ruby-crown kinglet whose constant melodies brighten the immediate vicinity beginning in late April and lasting through May. I have never found either bird to breed near houses, although they nest regularly in nearby boreal habitats.

Although winter is a time of want for birds in the Great South Woods, I maintain a regular slate of residents at this season. Their residency here is perhaps partially encouraged by the sunflower seeds I put out for them in their time of want. Birds whose presence I can consistently count on in winter are the black-capped chickadees, blue jays, red-breast nuthatches, white-breast nuthatches, downy woodpeckers, hairy woodpeckers, and ravens. The downy woodpecker and white-breasted nuthatch are less avid users of the feeder than the others. About a decade or so ago, mourning doves began to appear at the feeder in winter, perhaps encouraged by the generally warmer weather we had been experiencing. Along the same line, crows departed *en masse* from the Great South Woods in winter to travel a short distance to the farmlands of the St. Lawrence Valley, where they established winter roosts by the hundreds or more. Lately, however, some crows have been over-wintering here, and I hear them in back of the house. Is this to be another outcome of global warming? Stay tuned.

Purple finch and goldfinch also feed sporadically in small flocks here in winter. Unlike most of the other winter residents, they have a fondness for thistle seeds, and I engage them by providing them with this luxury at this season. The purple finch nests in the large white pines in front of the house, where their pleasant warble remains a treasured memory of the first month of my daughter's life, when this liquid burst of vocal sunshine appeared to be ever-present to brighten our days.

The sunflower seeds in winter occasionally manage to attract grouse to the vicinity, but it is a rare occasion indeed when they manage to entice wild turkey. This has happened on only two occasions, each for a few days at a time. Apparently, the preferred bill of fare for wild turkeys is corn, which may now be considered verboten, in one sense, as it is generally thought of as being winter food for deer.

Several "winter finches" arrive in visiting populations every few years. Redpolls and pine siskins are especially abundant, usually in alternate years. I have never seen them in large numbers in the same winter, however. Then there is the evening grosbeak, which, up to the mid-1990s, was abundant all through the winter. Lately, their winter populations have become far sparser. My thought is that birds have stopped migrating in response to conditions in the far north, and now we have to be mainly content with local breeding birds visiting our winter feeders,

Indisputably, there are also certain mammals that are attracted to human abodes. Raccoons and skunks are regularly seen in the vicinity of the house, although not on a year-round basis, since both species usually lie low during winter. Raccoons are primarily attracted to the garbage in

Photo courtesy Newcomb Visitors' Interpretive Center

A hopeful raccoon checks out the bird feeder.

bird feeders that invariably adorn human residences. Mine is no exception. Various grubs around the lawn and garden are the source of attraction for skunks. They especially reveal their activity by diggings in the sod in late summer and autumn.

Woodchucks are also on the scene, in spite of heavy predation from coyotes. They frequently utilize the culvert under the Route 3 roadway but also dig their own dens. At all times, though, they manage to wreak havoc on my vegetable garden. The only crops that seem to repel them are potatoes and tomatoes. Several years ago, I had an interesting experience with one of these critters I had surprised in a fenced-in portion of my garden. In its frantic panic to escape from me, it became wedged and wrapped in the lowest wire of the fence while attempting to dig under it. It made a noise similar to the sucking of a pump, and then it snapped at me with a sudden lunge. Once again, I became aware of the fury of a rodent.

Weasels have several times taken up residence under the attached garage. They no doubt have been lured here by the abundance of deer mice and shrews around the sunflower feeder in winter.

Snowshoe hares put in an appearance 12 years after the red pines were planted. They lasted about a decade before disappearing, probably because of the pines outgrowing their reach. They furnished some sport during their local tenure — and, more importantly, they never once touched my garden.

The sunflower feeder also lured gray squirrels and, I believe, has been instrumental in establishing them as permanent residents.

A brace of garter snakes and a few milk snakes have a communal den under the cement stoop on the side of the house. There is an even-larger den in an old dry well located directly across Route 3 from my house. From these dens, the serpents sally forth to search for prey in the sunshine. The hordes of crickets and grasshoppers swarming through the grasses of the lawn furnish ample food for smaller specimens of both these species. For larger garter snakes, frogs and toads seem to be the fare of the day. I have not noticed the larger milk snake hunting anything specifically, but a glance at the literature reveals that deer mice are probably at the top of the preferred menu here.

American toads and pickerel frogs hunt through the grass of the lawn. Like the smaller snakes, they, too, are waxing plentiful in this luscious place, getting fat on the prey that is always present in the grass. For my part, I keep grass cutting to a minimum to encourage this mini-version of an eastern prairie. Very occasionally, a northern leopard frog will be found in addition to the toads and pickerel frogs.

In two different winters, spotted salamanders, another amphibian species, has put in an appearance in my basement. I presume they have been lured there to hibernate, yet the two I found, on both occasions, were still active, albeit quite sluggish in movement.

The basement also plays host to deer mice and shrews in winter, and I would not be surprised if the weasel had not, on occasion, also entered the basement in anticipation of fine dining. Red squirrel and chipmunk frequently enter the garage, and several times the red squirrel has got into the basement. Chipmunks were totally absent from here when my neighbor's house cats were free-ranging, but now that they have been curbed, chipmunks have become abundant again, giving testimony to the powers of exotics in an ecosystem.

Flying squirrels, probably of the northern variety, have a nest in a large white pine nearby and regularly visit the sunflower feeder at night.

Insects, of course, are quite abundant around my house. Some are very welcome; others are not. The blooms of the lilac hedge are scanned avidly, beginning in mid-May, for the brilliantly adorned butterflies and moths that pollinate them. Joyous to behold, and intensely uplifting to the spirit, is the sight of massed tiger swallowtails and hummingbird moths frolicking among the lilac blossoms. Bumblebees, solitary bees, and other butterflies are also present and add to the delight of blossom watching. Later on, hummingbirds and several species of fritillaries arrive on the scene to grace the flower garden with their beauty.

Their loveliness and grace are not restricted to the daylight, as was dramatically revealed to me the night I left a light on over a side window of the house. When I looked out the window in the morning, there were hundreds of moths of a dozen species still clinging to the windows after being attracted there by the light. Infinite in their form and dazzling in their brilliance, they were truly a sight to behold. Virgin tiger moths, rosy maple moths, giant leopard moths, imperial moths, and underwing moths — all were present. Most common were the adult moth of the Eastern tent caterpillar and the forest tent caterpillar. This latter species had an outbreak of population in 2004 and seriously defoliated several hardwood trees. This encounter provokes me to ponder on the many jewels that fly at night, completely outside our knowledge or perception. The climax to this episode was the sight of chipping sparrows descending on the scene in a frenzy to pluck the hapless moths off the window. Such are some of the wonders of nature revealed around a homestead.

Wildlife Sights

In a heavily wooded area like the Adirondacks, where so many wildlife species have faced heavy persecution, most woodland inhabitants choose to remain hidden from the prying eyes of humans. The thick forests and the nocturnal habits of the majority of these creatures serve them admirably in this. One must infer their presence by observing their tracks and other signs, and be content just to know that they are there.

However, the law of averages dictates that a person spending a considerable amount of time in the woods is occasionally going to get some dramatic sightings of wildlife. This may be a glimpse of a charismatic, rare or "ghost" species — or, perhaps, a brief view of a more mundane life form acting in a most unusual fashion. It is these sightings that I most cherish and that lend a definite sparkle to living in the Great South Woods.

Some of my intimate sightings have been of various creatures of the wild interacting with each other. These sightings were varied in form and covered a broad range of species. For instance, I have twice witnessed does nursing fawns without knowing they were watched. Once, on the shores of the Raquette River, twin fawns were involved; in both instances, the fawns were mobile and not still in the helpless stage.

Once, while I was leading a nature walk at the Newcomb Visitors Interpretive Center, our group of nine rounded a bend in the forest trail and witnessed a great horned owl in the process of dismantling a ruffed grouse he had just dispatched. Needless to say, all were thrilled at this spectacle of raw nature unfolding.

On another occasion, I came upon a mob of crows verbally and physically harassing a lone great horned owl they had discovered sitting in a tree in daylight. How this poor owl was suffering for his sins! I frequently see redwing blackbirds dive-bombing red-tail hawks as they frantically attempt to escape them by flight. Both of these occurrences seemed to be in the spirit of defending the young or, perhaps, vengeance for some unseen offense.

At another time, I observed several blue jays calling as they attacked a mink ambling along the banks of a creek and endeavoring to ignore them. I had a clear vantage point from the crest of a hill, and the pageant unfolded before my eyes until the mink found shelter in a creek-side den. The notoriously bold blue jay is well known for his sauciness, a reputation that was certainly confirmed that day.

Another inter-species encounter I happened upon revolved around a bowl of cat food that had been placed outside my house. Inside the house, I was startled by a series of shrieks and growls just before the pungent odor of skunk wafted through the air and into the house. Apparently, a raccoon and a skunk had contested the contents of the bowl. When I went outside, I found the raccoon stranded on top of the garage, the skunk walking haughtily away. Imagine!

Still another example of inter-species strife that I came upon was miniscule in size, but not in the import it conveyed to me. It occurred about two decades ago on a sunny November afternoon while I was hunting the Blue Ridge Wilderness near Blue Mountain Lake. I sat down and rested my back against the trunk of a large hardwood tree and began to daydream. My musings were interrupted by the sight of two short-tailed shrews appearing suddenly about ten feet from where I was. The duo appeared to be doing a kind of choreographed dance with each other as they performed a type of duel that almost seemed to be played out according to Marquis of Queensbury rules. First one, then the other, would attempt to strike its opponent in a rather restrained fashion. The contest was devoid for all this time of any growling or other noises. All of a sudden, one of the shrews fell prone on the ground and began to twitch violently in a series of convulsions before becoming still and lifeless. The other shrew then proceeded to drag the inert one away.

This was too much for my curiosity, so I arose and approached closer for a better view. The victor quickly fled the scene. The first shrew was definitely dead, without any marks of violence whatsoever on the body. Everything was consistent with a death from poison, with the victor hauling the vanquished away for consumption in a more secure setting. The stylized ritual dueling I had observed was each shrew trying meticulously to insert his poison saliva into the other. I considered these proceedings to be particularly significant because at that time, two decades ago, I had in my possession a relatively recently published wildlife manual that questioned strongly whether in fact a short-tail shrew possessed any poisonous saliva. After what I had just witnessed, it was difficult to prevent a touch of smugness from descending upon me. It also buttressed my conviction that more could be learned concerning the habits and even the existence of creatures of the wild by observation in the field than by compiling notes in an office.

The now-ubiquitous raven has been the center of many of the species interactions that have unfolded before my eyes. In winter, we have the spectacle of ravens interacting with bald eagles and coyotes around the locale of deer carcasses. The ravens watch the coyotes for the site of a kill; the eagles hone in on the ravens for the same reason, then chase the ravens away from the carcass. The ravens hover on the periphery of the site and, if the eagles are unwary, dash in at a moment's notice.

During the non-winter months, ravens frequently interact with turkey vultures at the site of road kills. This is especially noticeable at sunrise or shortly after. I have seen a raven directly attack and drive away a turkey vulture at a cliff nest on Cat Mountain.

Reverting back to the intra-species level, I have noticed pairs of beavers grooming each other on several occasions, always on land. The grooming was quite deliberate, even meticulous; and in all cases, the animals were so absorbed in their activity they were unaware of my presence.

Perhaps the most curious habit of all wildlife sightings was that epic I call "the foxes of the fairway." For several years, the Clifton Fine Municipal Golf Course in Star Lake was home to a family of rather tame foxes who exhibited a most curious habit. The young foxes would often run after and retrieve the struck golf balls and promptly bring them back to their den, which was located on the fairway. This bizarre yet amusing habit furnished enjoyment to local golfers, who were very protective of the foxes.

On a number of occasions, I have had encounters with wildlife that might best be described as hostile in nature. One of these involved a beaver crossing a dirt road at dusk in the Silver Lake State Forest. After I left my car, the beaver approached me in a threatening manner and appeared to be snapping at me. I quickly re-entered the car and drove off. Several old-time trappers have since informed me they have had similar incidents with beavers. I feel that a contributing factor to this behavior could be the heightened sense of vulnerability beavers undoubtedly feel when on land.

A similar incident with an Eastern coyote occurred while I was driving on Tooly Pond Road one bright August afternoon. A young, three-quarter-grown coyote was standing at the side of the road. When I stopped my vehicle and went outside for a closer look, the coyote, instead of fleeing, began to walk slowly right toward me. When he approached to within 15 feet without stopping, I let discretion overcome valor and re-entered my vehicle. The coyote then turned and trotted slowly off. I have often pondered this incident in moments when my mind was not fully engaged otherwise. I can only deduce that, since the young coyote showed no outright signs of aggression, perhaps this was just a case of foolish curiosity on the part of the immature canine. I do have to wonder, however, how long he survived with such behavior.

Another incident of an antagonistic encounter was related in the first volume of *The Great South Woods*. While I was on a breeding-bird survey, a muskrat actually attacked and bit my rubber boots. I attributed this random occurrence to the early hour (before sunrise) and to the unexpectedness of the encounter on the part of the muskrat.

The rationale for an attack by an ermine that was protecting its food supply was much more obvious. At the crack of dawn, I had come upon a ermine with two red-back voles in his mouth. It was spring, and the weasel was no doubt bringing the voles back to the den as food for its young. Upon seeing me approaching, the ermine dropped the prey and disappeared into a small fissure approximately thirty feet away while I went on to examine his two prey items. After the briefest of intervals, the ermine popped his head straight out of the burrow and ran straight at me, chattering all the while. I discreetly withdrew; the weasel retrieved its prey, then proceeded jauntily along to its home den. This is a classic example of extended mammal protectiveness toward their young.

Over the years, I have been visited repeatedly at a campsite in the evening by black bears and martens, particularly bears. The visits have occurred while I was staying both in pup tents and at lean-tos. The *raison d'être* for these nocturnal visits, of course, was a search for food on the part of the woodland denizens, not a desire to manifest any hostility.

Still, a few of the encounters with bears were somewhat harrowing, particularly with one bear who was inordinately persistent. Two bear incidents that spring readily to mind are that of the bear that attempted to roll me over in my sleeping bag on the banks of the Oswegatchie, and the other about another bear that doggedly refused to leave the vicinity of our lean-to, despite all our endeavors to induce him to do so. Hollering at the top of my lungs persuaded the first bear to flee, while only the emergence of dawn convinced the second one that he had overstayed his welcome.

Finally, every once in an eon, it seems a sighting is made of a creature so regal and rare that the soul is uplifted for hours, even days. Some of these are of creatures rare enough to make their very existence in the Great South Woods amazing. Into this category would fit both the moose cow and calf I sighted in 1983 and the Canada lynx spied in 1977. Both sightings are detailed in the first Great South Woods. Fitting even more snugly in this category are sightings I made of the wolverine in 2003 and of the two "Eastern" or red wolves in 2004. Just to be afforded a glimpse of one of these magnificent creatures is, I believe, ample reason to thank the Creator.

Photo by Uta Wister

Another WILDLIFE SIGHT from before our time ....

The Caribou

Did you know? According to recent findings, the regal Caribou roamed across the St. Lawrence River to the northern Adirondacks until several centuries ago.

8
GREAT SOUTH WOODS CALENDAR

The natural calendar of the Great South Woods usually proceeds in a somewhat orderly progression, with one season blending subtly into the next. This blending, however, is often variable, with areas of overlap depending mainly on the weather conditions of that year. In conformance with this weather pattern, the time of emergence may be early or late; but the sequence of emergence almost invariably remains the same.

The projected forecast of global warming may skew this calendar in the future. Indeed, this may already be happening, as the annual appearance of birds, insects, blossoms, and leaves seems to be occurring much earlier, according to the nature diary I have maintained for 30 years.

It should also be kept in mind that, while there is no such thing as a "typical" year, a pattern of occurrence can still be easily observed by keeping track of the years. The events listed here are all personal observations made down through the years.

Initially, I had to deal with the question of where to start the calendar. After some thought, I decided it should start with the waking up of the woods in March of each year.

Sucker Bridge Stream

Photos courtesy Newcomb Visitors' Interpretive Center

MARCH

"In like a lion and out like a lamb" is a folk wisdom that has often been applied to March. However, the exact converse of this can occasionally apply. I have experienced a number of years when March entered like a lamb only to exit like the king of the beasts. This aptly illustrates the changing nature of March weather.

The first early harbinger of spring that I invariably see is the returning redwing blackbirds and grackles who put in an appearance by mid-March, when the ground is still mantled by a covering of snow. Robins arrive a little later. The redwings, all male, manage to cheer up forlorn winter days with their caroling at this time. Robins usually do not begin singing until a week or so later. Several birds that have remained all winter now commence their breeding. Included here are ravens, gray jays, and great horned owls. Ravens are especially vocal in March, making a varied repertory of sound. Snowy conditions and still-frigid cold appear not to discourage these avian procreators in the least. Raccoons now tentatively begin to make an appearance, seemingly freed from their winter torpor. Their mini-bear-like tracks are often reflected in the snow as they wander widely in pursuit of food and passion. Crows, having just returned from their temporal abode in the St. Lawrence Valley, also begin to call early in the a.m. This is just about the time the "winter finches" begin to return to their arctic breeding grounds.

Much bare ground usually begins to appear in the latter part of March. Wild turkeys and white-tail deer are now a regular sight as they feed on the newly revealed grass at roadsides. This grass, however old, is a welcome respite from the meager fare of winter. March even brings forth the occasional butterfly in the form of the Compton tortoise shell. This attractive, white-marked butterfly is erratic in appearance and seemingly does not fly every year. On those years when it does appear, I generally see the first ones in March.

Finally, March is the premier month for the shining displays of the aurora borealis or northern lights. These mysterious lights, caused by electro-magnetic fields, illuminate the entire sky with their shimmering, greenish hues on select March evenings.

Star Flower

Forest floor in spring

Photos by Nadine McLaughlin

April

When the proverbial April showers arrive, the transition to spring is well underway. The weather can still be mercurial, and snow is not unheard of, but the process of the annual renewal of the landscape is now irreversible.

Mud and water is everywhere, which is aptly illustrated by the cresting rivers and streams as they run far too high for any reasonable trout fishing on opening day. They also destroy many of last year's beaver dams by washing them out, facilitating an ease of paddling from now until the beavers reconstruct the dams. Black bears are out of hibernation now, and their sign is seen once again as they ravenously seek food after their winter's fast. I often see moose tracks in April, as these huge cervids disperse from their upland conifer yarding areas of winter to seek the solitude of lakes and beaver ponds until the autumn rutting season.

The nocturnal calls of mating frogs are a regular feature of those April evenings. The calling amphibians, all males, are now in a breeding frenzy, as the ubiquitous call of the spring peepers attests, its volume progressively increasing as April wears on. The peepers' chorus is by far the loudest, but there are several other frogs that actually precede them with more subtle and singular calls of the April evenings. I usually hear the quack-like call of wood frogs several days before the peepers commence their nocturnal serenades. The low call of the leopard frog also arrives earlier than the peepers, but I have found this amphibian to be more common in the St. Lawrence Valley than in the Great South Woods. The call of the chorus frog, which I also hear on rare occasions, is similarly restricted to the St. Lawrence Valley. Looking under woodland stones and logs may reveal the presence of a salamander. This is the seldom-seen, red-backed salamander, which is actually one of the most common vertebrates in the Great South Woods.

April is the month that heralds the arrival of the birds of summer. Their migration will climax in May, but April still brings forth the first hermit thrushes, winter wrens, solitary vireo and sapsuckers, among others. Their songs and calls resonate and bring a touch of life to the still April woods. I have seen the winter wren building a nest as early as the first week of April, and by mid-April the discordant hammering of the sapsuckers in hollow trees is a regular feature of the diurnal April chorus.

One bird song of April, that of the purple finch, evokes treasured memories whenever I hear it. In 1974, my wife and I brought our daughter, Carmen, barely one week old, up to the house in Fine. It was mid-April, and for a full month the pleasant warbles of a purple finch serenaded us from the top of a large white pine in front of the house. This particular finch sang constantly from daybreak to sundown. At the time, I felt this was something special; and despite the passage of over three decades, I still feel this way.

Ruby-crown kinglets give forth their distinctive trills in April. They hold forth in song for several weeks but do not breed here. The closest I have found them breeding is in the vicinity of Streeter Lake.

The woodcocks have also returned by April. They have several varied and unusual sounds that manage to liven up the twilight of a dull April day.

Turkey vultures have arrived by April, too, and may be seen continually soaring in the sky on the lookout for dead deer or any other form of carrion lying below.

The goshawk, a true emblem of the big woods, is actively proceeding with nest building now. They are very protective of their young, and on three different occasions I have had to retreat from the vicinity of one of their nests after experiencing what could only be described as a full-blown attack from one of these fearless raptors.

Mallards and wood ducks have returned to their breeding haunts by now, as has the American bittern with his eerie, booming calls that reverberate through the marsh.

A number of butterflies are now present. Especially notable at this time are the mourning cloak and several species of comma, which have all over-wintered as adults and now fly forth in search of flowing sap and mammal scat, items that sustain them in their breeding endeavors.

Some early blossoms do not believe in waiting for May to send forth their floral offerings. Adder's tongue, spring beauty, and red trillium all begin to hold sway now. Added to these are hepaticas, Dutchmen's breeches, and squirrel corn, all growing in areas that have a rich, more-neutral soil.

Their pollinators are now out and about, also. Flesh flies tend to pollinate red trillium, attracted by their carrion-like scent. All these other blossoms are pollinated by a dazzling variety of solitary native bees and "bee-flies," which imitate the bees in color and form as a means of securing protection from predators. These insects can be found flying low to the ground on early spring mornings as they search for the blooms. These bees, mostly of halictid and andrenid lineage, then fly back to their tiny nest mounds, which have their small entrance holes on top. There they feed the pollen and honey to their young.

These industrious insects, however, have a legion of imitators that mimic them physically so as to secure entrance to their dens, where they then lay their eggs with the sole purpose of parasitizing the young of the honest "toilers." These parasites are also mainly bees and flies. Look carefully in early spring, and you'll be surprised at their variety.

I also see a native "white butterfly" at this time as it performs its pollinating routine. These "whites," which are either the mustard white or West Virginia white, have largely been replaced over most of the northeast by the exotic cabbage white.

A few trees send forth their blossoms in April. The cardinal-like haze shimmering on hillsides is from the blossoms of the red maple, while the pale catkins waving in the breeze belong to the aspen. Both of these early flowering trees are pollinated mainly by wind, but I also frequently see ruffed grouse feeding on the aspen catkins high in the trees in April.

April now sends forth the first true leaves. These come primarily on box alders and occasionally on lilacs. Both of these are exotic species, as is the tartarian honeysuckle, which also comes into leaf in April. I misguidedly planted the above in the 1970s as "wildlife food" after securing the seedlings from the Federal Soil and Water Conservation District. I now very much regret this; but this scenario was very much in vogue several decades ago, before the full impact of exotic species was realized.

One tree that is native to our area, however, now sends forth its leaves. As April grades into May, miniature leaves of black cherry begin to wave in the breeze, a harbinger of May and things to come.

Conifer-clad shoreline

Photo by Uta Wister

Photo by Nadine McLaughlin

Babbling brook in May

May

The proverbial "flowers of May" certainly becomes a truism in the Great South Woods. The early blooms that begin in April continue on to their full glory in May. Many of these early joys are spring vernals that have to set forth their flowers before the forest leaf canopy is out in full. Their leaves then mostly wither away by early summer, as their food and energy for next year's advent is now stored in their roots and bulbs.

Many others now join these early blossoms as the forest's floral display now comes into its full glory. Painted trillium and bellwort now appear, just as the earlier blooms begin to wane. For a short time, all are blooming simultaneously. The butter yellow of cowslip now livens up the swamp, while the nutrient-rich upland soils that are often adjacent to the cowslip's soil produce the subtle greenish flowers of cohosh, while the pungent leaves of wild leek advertise their presence. This is a good place to find the more uncommon spring vernals. Toward the end of the month, bunchflowers and Canada mayflowers adorn the forest floor with their splendid blossoms. The bunchflower is actually a dwarf dogwood, while the Canada mayflower grows as a colony of clones that carpet the woodlands as May draws to a close.

While the Great South Woods lack the spectacular blossoms of azaleas and rhododendrons found in the Smoky Mountains and other southern regions, they do manage to have their own gorgeous floral displays from several small trees and shrubs inhabiting their edges and openings. These include the shadberry, pin cherry, and hobblebush, all of which have attractive white blossoms. The shadberry is first to bloom, followed closely by the more subtle blossoms of the pin cherry. Hobblebush, a wild viburnum, is the last of the trio to bloom and displays more showy flowers than the other two. When I first arrived in the Great South Woods, hobblebush usually did not commence to bloom until the flowers of the other two had withered. Now, however, as a consequence of hobblebush blooming earlier, I often come upon all three woody plants blossoming simultaneously. Whether this can be attributed to global warming or to a normal oscillation in weather patterns, I do not know.

The leafing out of the overstory trees is now progressing along with the canopy, which is usually being fully leafed out by the third week of May. White ash and beech are the last trees to be adorned with leaves, and by this time there is a veritable army of ravenous insects present, mainly caterpillars, to munch on the unfurling leaves. Right in tandem with the caterpillars' is the arrival of the returning migrant birds to greet the insects. Up to a score of species of warblers are especially adept at gleaning caterpillars off the tree leaves and converting them into energy for breeding.

That horror of the north, the black fly, first makes its presence known at this time, also, although lately they have been emerging earlier in May. 2004 was a year in which black flies were barely to be seen. Again, whether this was due to global warming, BTI spraying, or simply a natural fluctuation in numbers is unknown at this time.

The long trill of the American toad is now heard in the vicinity of water as male toads attempt to entice females for the purpose of breeding. Occasionally, I see the actual breeding itself, the smaller male toad clinging determinedly to a much-larger female as they plod along on land. Garter snakes now begin to be seen, too, often preying on these same toads.

Several common fish species are inspired by the arrival of May to commence breeding. The creek chub, with its loud nocturnal splashing in tiny creeks, presents an enchanting scene at this time. Large common suckers are run upstream to breed now. I vividly recall being part of a fishing expedition sometime during the 1970s, when we speared these rather tasty morsels. The locale was one of the minor creeks emptying into the Oswegatchie River near Wanakena.

The drummings of the courting male ruffed grouse seems to emanate from every woodland covert now. Broadwing hawks, the most common Adirondack raptor, can be seen perched in trees and telephone wires as they avidly gaze below for prey in the form of small mammals and reptiles. The dawn bird chorus is now in full swing, although much muted on the occasional still-chilly day. Chilly days, however, will not stifle the loud warning calls of ospreys on their nests. The ospreys, which returned in April, have waited until May to become so vocal in the vicinity of their nests. I look forward to hearing their cries and calls as May grades into June.

June

Several butterflies that made their appearance in May now become more common in June. The contrasting flights of the large Canada tiger swallowtail and the tiny spring azure are a source of visual delight well into the month. The flights of several other butterflies are also very noticeable now. One of these is the handsomely patterned white admiral which, in addition to being seen in flight, is also often noted feeding on coyote scat and around dried-up puddles along trails. In these instances, the admirals are probably seeing the salts in the scat and mud as an aid to their breeding efforts. Another strikingly attired butterfly that is commonly observed throughout June is the Atlantis fritillary. The fritillary is a frequent pollinator of the showy blossoms of June, thus securing their sustenance in a more orthodox fashion than the white admiral.

As June rolls on, the insect tribes wax to their zenith. Fireflies light up meadows and lawns with pinpricks of fire flashing in all directions. Different colors of flashing light and different intervals of flashing indicate a diversity of species. Dragonflies are now out in abundance. Three species of skimmers are especially notable around small lakes and beaver ponds. They are the elegantly named 10-spot skimmer, white-tail skimmer and Julia skimmer. In some years, they literally swarm all over, while in other years they are relatively scarce. But even in years of sparse population, they are always present to some degree.

The unsightly nests of tent caterpillars now put in an appearance, especially on branches of cherry and apple trees. The nests confer a measure of protection for the caterpillars and appear to make them relatively immune to predators. Still, they never appear to kill individual trees, although they do denude the branches. Every dozen or so years witnesses the outbreak of a forest tent caterpillar infestation. These relatives of the annual tent caterpillar feed primarily on aspen and maple and do, in fact, cause the death of individual trees. This occurs when they totally defoliate a tree without there being adequate time for the tree to re-grow a second growth of leaves before the advent of frost. 2004 was a year of forest tent caterpillar outbreak. It was also the first time in many years I have seen their main predators, two species of cuckoo, locally. It makes me ponder the intricacies of nature to wonder how the cuckoos could have arrived here so soon after the outbreak, when normally they are not present locally at all. The glories of the Creator are awesome!

Black flies, which first emerged in May, reach the pinnacle of their bloodthirstiness in June before finally subsiding toward the end of the month. There is only partial relief, however, since the deerfly, which first puts in an appearance in early June, now proliferates as the month progresses, replacing the black fly as the number one tormentor of mankind in the Great South Woods. Hot, sunny days seem to have been created solely for the purpose of vexing mankind by bestowing the horrors of the deerfly profusely on all and sundry.

The last two woodland wild flowers arrive on the scene in June in the person of the pink lady slipper and the wood sorrel. The former is an orchid, often growing under conifers. It is quite common here and is pollinated primarily by bumblebees. Digging it up and transplanting it, in addition to being illegal, is also usually quite useless, since the roots of the orchid depend on an intricate relationship with the mycelium of specific fungal species in order to secure enough nutrients from the soil to assure survival. Wood sorrel, which is related to the shamrock, remains in flower for a good part of the summer, unlike pink lady slippers, which burst forth in glory only to soon subside.

The frog chorus culminates in June with the nocturnal calls of bullfrogs, green frogs, and mink frogs resonating across the stillness of the night. Marshes, ponds, and lakes play host to this trio of large frogs, which continue calling, albeit at a lower volume, for much of the summer. The first two frogs are ubiquitous over the eastern part of the country, but the mink frog is a boreal specialist whose calls are heard nowhere south of the Adirondacks. The rapid trill of the diminutive tree frog concludes the nocturnal amphibian serenade. Tree frogs have a tendency to call when humidity is high, often preceding a summer storm. For this reason, the few farmers still remaining on the periphery of the Great South Woods when I arrived here regularly referred to these frogs as "rain frogs." I found they were usually correct.

June is also the time for spawning of bass. The spawning beds can often be seen as mounds in shallow ponds and lakes in our region. Originally, they were absent from the Adirondack uplands but were present in areas peripheral to the Great South Woods. They are now in enough local lakes to allow the bass season to open on June 15, making it a significant date for fishermen.

Finally, June is the month of fawns. Born in the end of May or early June, they begin to move about significantly and are seen for the first time after the middle of the month. On occasional, especially blissful days, they may even be seen nursing from the doe that bore them.

Photo by Nadine McLaughlin

White-tail family in early summer

Photo courtesy Newcomb Visitors' Interpretive Center

Peninsula Trail Lookout at the Newcomb VIC

July

The tempo of change and rising diversity calms down and becomes less frantic in July as summer arrives in its fullness. This slowing of earth's pace is best illustrated by the fading of the songs of breeding birds and the fading of the spring blossoms.

Red-eye vireo and eastern wood peewees are now the only birds usually in song, with the monotonous two-part call of the vireo reverberating all through a sultry summer day. Toward the middle of the month, cedar waxwings commence to breed, but their vocalizations are relatively muted.

Dewdrops now bloom profusely under the hardwood canopy, while the elegant goldthread becomes more numerous under the conifers. Elderberry blossoms, gorgeous to the sight, now brighten up the vicinity of marshes and beaver ponds. Joe Pye weed comes into flower in these areas now also. Look for its purple blossoms along rivers and marshes.

A large, strikingly colored butterfly, the great spangled fritillary, is often noticed pollinating the flowers of the Joe Pye weed at this time. Their orange coloring adds nicely to the purple blossoms of the flowers to create a pleasing image not soon forgotten.

Another gorgeous butterfly, the Baltimore, is seen in the vicinity of the turtlehead, which is also a wetland plant. The Baltimore, which is named after the colonial colors of Lord Baltimore, is unique in having its larvae restricted to the leaves of the turtlehead for sustenance. No turtlehead, no Baltimore!

A myriad of flying moths now appear as pinpricks of lighting to liven up the night. Their cryptic colors are often in somber hues, as befit nocturnal dalliers; but just as often these moths are adorned in dramatic hues. A light left on over a window will attract, among others, the following jewels of the evening: rosy maple moths, imperial moths, giant leopard moths, virgin tiger moths, etc. Their names are as flamboyant as their colors! Morning will still find them clinging to the outside walls, there to often be devoured by the birds of sunlight. The lunar moth and the io moth are the two most prominent of the giant silk moths that I see. Now is their time also!

The deerfly is at its most horrendous in July; but this is partially compensated for by the cessation of the black fly scourge as the month draws to a close. I have noticed, however, that a second species of black fly appears to emerge in July. This is mostly in boreal areas where conifers are dominant. The Oswegatchie River above Inlet is prone to this particular horror all through the month.

The explosion of dragonflies finds them doing their best to cope with catching the flies; but they are not able to totally eliminate the pests. A half dozen or more species of "emeralds" are among the most numerous of the dragonflies. These dragonflies, many of which have metallic green on their bodies, are a specialty of the Great South Woods and other boreal areas.

Families of otters are now often noted along the rivers. Often, they are in a frolicsome mood, which makes them a special delight to observe. Young snowshoe hares begin to put in an appearance, too. They have several broods a year, but this is the month when I most often observe them.

Finally, garter snakes become more frequently seen along the hiking trails as they hunt for American toads that have left the water to lead a terrestrial existence. This is also the month when painted turtles love to sun themselves on logs and boulders in or adjacent to bodies of still water.

A beaver house brings change to the environment.

Photo courtesy Newcomb Visitors' Interpretive Center

August

August continues the torpor of July as far as new sightings and arrivals go. Life is full, and many people enjoy the fullness by being relatively inactive.

Young coyotes and red foxes now appear along the grassy highway roadsides of the Great South Woods. They are attracted there by the numerous grasshoppers and crickets, now in full chorus. The inexperienced juvenile canines become road casualties almost as frequently as do the two insects.

Toward the middle of the month, the "chucking" sounds of chipmunks at their nests begin to resonate throughout the forest. Such a relatively loud sound for such a mite of a mammal! A little later, the solitary "peeps" of spring peepers begins to be heard coming from high up in trees. Mating completed, these tiny frogs have left the water and become true tree frogs.

Later on in the month, wild turkeys are found in large numbers feeding at roadsides or in the fields of the few remaining farms. Several hens combine their broods now. I have seen as many as 40 turkeys in local flocks in August. The goldfinch is the last bird to nest and may now be seen in open areas locally. Their striking yellow plumage and distinctive rolling flight call add spice to the dog days of August.

By the middle of August, the horrors wrought by deerfly have finally begun to abate, and rambling along forest trails becomes even more pleasurable. A much more pleasant replacement begins to appear in the form of the gorgeously attired monarch butterflies that have recently arrived after a long sojourn in southerly regions, where their forebears had migrated the year before.

Native wild flowers are now generally restricted to the vicinity of wetlands. The aptly named cardinal flower lends a touch of brilliance along area streams and rivers for almost the entire month. The indigo blue of closed gentians similarly lights up area marshes and the edges of fens.

August is the month when a dazzling variety of mushrooms springs forth on the forest floor, usually in response to late-summer rains. Some of the more notable fungi are russula, amanita, destroying angel, and boletes, their colors ranging from red and yellow to purple and brown.

Finally, August plays host to what is probably the premier sky spectacle of the entire calendar year. This takes place in the form of the Perseus Meteor Shower, which I usually spy during the second week of the month, concurrent with the time when the first howlings of young coyotes are heard. I thrill to both!

The gardens are winding down, the sunflowers grown tall.

Photo by Nadine McLaughlin

SEPTEMBER

September in our area starts out as a time of transition but soon progresses, usually rapidly, to autumn. Soon comes the period of the fall foliage spectacle, which begins around the middle of the month.

The turning of the leaves of the red maple from green into a glorious cardinal red heralds the start of this annual pageant. Very shortly thereafter, white ash leaps into maroon and purple foliage. Leaves of a purplish color adorn the leaves of hobblebush in the forest understory. Black chokeberry adds another dash of red in open wet areas. All these species are the early harbingers of fall, with their glorious pinnacle of color usually reached in the last week in September. This zenith of glory culminates in the brilliant golden orange of sugar maples and the shimmering gold of yellow birch. For the past half-decade or so, however, this crowning glory has been postponed until early October. While this delaying of fall foliage turnover may be attributable to global climate change, I am earnestly hoping it is only temporary and a mere normal fluctuation in weather patterns.

September is the time of moose. It is now that bull moose begin their rut and commence to wander freely in search of cow moose. It never ceases to amaze me how an animal the size of a moose can remain solitary and secretive in the vicinity of local wetlands all through the summer, only becoming evident now at the time of their annual frenzied mating rambles.

Several mammals that are complete hibernators are seen for the last time now. Roadside woodchucks fit into this category, as do both species of jumping mice, which are seldom seen because of their nocturnal habits.

Black cherry fruiting, which began in August, continues unabated in its falling from trees, later to be utilized by a variety of forest creatures. This is reflected in the scat of black bears and coyotes, which for a period of several weeks in September consists primarily of fruit. Earlier in the month, some of the fruit is still that of the blackberry, although its tasty morsels are mainly consumed in August.

Kestrels are a common sight on transmission wires along roadsides in September. Small flocks of robins and flickers are noted here also, as they gorge themselves on wild fruits preparatory to their departure for southern climes.

Monarch butterflies, after just a short interlude here, begin to return south in great numbers. These massive aggregations are a stunning sight not soon to be forgotten when they are occasionally glimpsed.

Paper wasps are now frequently seen on the walls of houses. These are the queen wasps that will hibernate inside walls at this time, to awaken the following spring to establish new colonies. I find them quite striking in form as well as habit and begrudge them not in the least the use of my abode for their winter slumber.

The Bog River in Autumn.

Photo by Nadine McLaughlin

October

The fall foliage show, which reaches its apex in the northern hardwood forest, continues its progression in October. In fact, the very peak of this progression has been attained in October for the past five years or so. This peak period is highlighted by the brilliant colors of sugar maples and yellow birch supplemented by the subtle drab browns of beeches, which blend nicely into the background. As these leaves wither and fall, they are supplanted along about mid-October by the shining yellows of aspen and tamarack, which have waited until now to send forth their coloring. This final blast of glory is a prelude to the dropping of the leaves, at which period the tree canopy will become somber and silent for another seven months.

Beavers are now very much in evidence as they cut trees for their winter food cache, which they place in the underwater mud next to their lodges. They are less furtive now, and are thus observed more frequently.

Skunks are also more active now, and the round diggings they make for insects can often be seen on area lawns. This increased feeding activity is a precursor to the torpor or semi-hibernation state they undergo in winter.

The end of September usually witnesses the last sight of chipmunks before they go into their winter hibernation. Yet, in early October they are still often seen as they scurry about in pursuit of beechnuts, cherry fruit, and other mast to store with them in their winter abodes.

Brook trout ascend headwater streams now to breed in gravelly areas. The last garter snakes of the year are in evidence, usually sunning themselves before entering their communal hibernation dens for the winter.

The yellowish sulphur is the last butterfly of the year to make an appearance, but still quite common early in the month.

The last dragonflies to be seen are the blue darner and the smaller meadowflies. There are several species of each, and they fade from sight at approximately the same time as the sulphurs disappear for the year.

The large, globular nests of bald-face hornets are now commonly observed hanging from leafless tress before the winds of winter consign them to oblivion. Hordes of dead workers may still be seen inside, but the queen has departed to hibernate nearby. She will not awaken until it is time to begin a new brood the following spring.

Wooly bear caterpillars become a frequent sight as they amble along the ground before entering their hibernation. After they awaken in the spring, they will alter their form and become a rather drab-appearing moth.

Red-tail hawks now haunt the vicinity of trees at roadsides. They will stay around until the snow cover becomes deep enough to obscure the small voles they utilize for prey.

Not so the loons, which are off on the wings of the early hard frosts to seek sustenance in ice-free waters farther south. For me, when their eerie calls have ceased reverberating across our area's lakes, it spells the death knell of the natural year..

Yellow birch growing on glacial eratic

Photo courtesy Newcomb Visitors' Center

NOVEMBER

November, to me, is a somber, sullen month with the trees finally devoid of all leaves except lifeless beech leaves that persist in clinging to the branches throughout the entire winter. The ground now appears to be ready to welcome the snow cover that is coming. The only relief is provided by the occasional "Indian summer" day, when even ruffed grouse are deceived into going into their spring drumming ritual. Great blue herons are often conspicuous now as they fly from one unfrozen pond to the next. They will not leave until a cover of ice is upon all area waters.

November is the peak of the rut of white-tail deer, and the normally furtive bucks now throw caution to the winds in their frenzied quest for receptive does. Scrapes and buck rubs are now seen in the forest again. Bears are feeding voraciously in preparation for their winter slumber. Their "nests," evidence of feeding on mast in black cherry and beech trees, are now observed in the tops of the trees. These "nests" are seen less often now in beech as many mature trees succumb to beech-scale disease.

Insect life is definitely now at a premium. I often see a species of midge swarming in its up-and-down flight patterns, which are indicators of mating. There is also a smallish, light-brown moth, constantly flying in a fluttering fashion on bright, sunshiny days, and I often remember vividly the old-time hunters referring to these moths as "buck moths." Since a moth species called buck moth is on the state endangered species list, I became very impressed with the fact that these flittery moths are something special and more common than the experts thought. Alas, I learned later on that such was not the fact. The true endangered buck moth was a species restricted mostly to pine barrens downstate, while our common "buck moth" is merely the recipient of a colloquial appellation bestowed on them by hopeful hunters as they ardently pursued their prey.

Traditionally, old-time trappers proclaimed that a cold snap would get the "fur moving." In a strong sense, this is true as cool November days do seem to coincide with a pattern of greater activity among a number of carnivores. At this time of year, I probably see more mink and fisher abroad than at any other time of the year. Sights of these two mustelids are always rather rare, but definitely seem to be increasing now. An indisputable fact, for with these cold snaps and the "movement of the fur," winter is truly just over in the next forest glade!

Photo by Uta Wister

Barred Owl in late autumn

December

December is usually the start of the deep winter freeze. Deer now begin to go to their "yards," or winter concentration areas. These are low-lying conifer sections where the animals receive some relief from both wind and snow depth. Deer are often sighted en route to these areas, which may be ten miles or more from their summer range.

This is also the month of hibernating for most black bears. Females with young are the first to den, while old males are the last to enter their winter sanctuary. I have, on a number of occasions, noticed male bears up and around until the very end of December.

The Spartan conditions of December usually translate to a sparse bird presence. If there is any open water on the larger lakes, a few pairs of common mergansers may be heard. An occasional barred owl may yet call on still evenings or cloudy afternoons. Some goshawks have fled south, but others are still in the area. Completely silent now, they are sometimes spotted flying purposefully across forest openings.

The many species of fungi that live in the Great South Woods are now revealed by their fruiting bodies on the bark of trees. Some of these are polypores that can be seen continually for a number of years, while other species occur but are only in evidence for a period of a few months. I often point out and discuss these fungi, as well as tree lichens, on days when I lead winter walks at the Newcomb Visitors Interpretive Center. When the snow tracking is non-existent, an interest in the fascinating variety and aspects of these life forms can be kindled in many an observer. Among the more readily observed now are turkey-tail, tinder conk, false tinder conk, artist conk, birch polypore, red-belt polypore, plus a dazzling variety of others. As stated before, their ecologies and lifestyles are as fascinating as their names.

Winter at Rich Lake

Nature trail foot bridge at Newcomb VIC.

Photos courtesy Newcomb Visitors' Interpretive Center

January

January is truly the time of deep freeze. The migrants are all gone, the hibernators are slumbering, and only the truly hardy are abroad. It is only within the past several years that I've seen the ground not snow covered, albeit then only for a short time.

Harsh as is the January climate, it is also the time when some avian wanderers arrive here to partially replace the local birds that have fled. These sojourners are primarily winter finches that are fleeing a period of even greater want in Arctic Canada. They now join our local winter-hardy birds in sampling the delights of winter bird feeders. These "winter finches" are quite erratic in their appearances, and there may be intervals of several years between sightings of them. In fact, some of the interludes in which they are absent in winter may stretch to half a decade. White-winged crossbills and red crossbills are in this category, although both of these conifer specialists have small local breeding populations also. Pine siskins are similar in habits. After a particularly heavy winter influx of the birds, some of them will remain behind in spring to breed here. Redpolls also come down; but as far as I know, they have not bred in the Great South Woods. The evening grosbeak is one of the "winter finches" that seem to be present on a regular basis in winter. In some years, their populations are sparse and may consist of only birds that bred locally. As well as sunflower seeds, they are attracted to the keys of box elders, which hang on the trees all winter.

Regular local birds that are present in winter include red-breast and white-breast nuthatches, hairy and downy woodpeckers, purple finches, chickadees, and blue jays. The sunflower seeds in feeders attract them all, while suet provides an extra inducement to bring both kinds of woodpeckers around. I find the presence of all these avian jewels definitely enhances the quality of life during winter in the Great South Woods.

Moose are now generally confined to small areas of upland conifers where they gather in small aggregations. This is in direct contrast to deer, which usually are far more abundant in their winter concentration areas. Even with these small moose numbers, however, the damage to the conifers from their feeding, which can be seen after the winter has passed, is something to behold.

Winter is the time I also see small aggregations of flying squirrels huddling together in communal nests for greater warmth, hoping to ward off the chills of the season. All of the flying squirrels I have seen have been of the northern species, although the southern flying squirrel is also present at lower population levels.

An Adirondack stream in winter.

Photo courtesy Newcomb Visitors' Interpretive Center

February

This month begins as a continuation of January. The winter raptors that have flown here from the north in response to vole prey cycles seem to be more in evidence in February. Rough-legged hawks and snowy owls glide over open areas on the periphery of the Adirondack Park. Hawk owls and great gray owls may be found in wooded areas, but they are even more rare than the first two raptors mentioned. All of these avian predators, even the owls, fly during the daytime and are easily seen on the rare occasions when they are present. This diurnal flight results mainly from the fact that these raptors are still adhering to an Arctic schedule when they are present in the Great South Woods.

The tempo of mammal activity begins to pick up its pace during February. Porcupines are often seen sitting and feeding in trees during the daytime. Frequently they are found in hemlock trees; and the cut branches that litter the ground provide an appetizing bonus for hungry deer and hares.

Foxes are paired up by now, and their tracks in the snow reflect this. They are also seen more often at this time due to their increased hunting activities as breeding season unfolds.

Bobcats, too, are in the midst of mating activity; and the fearsome yowls of the male seeking a female resounds through the stillness of an evening, imparting a note of mystery and even hazard to the night.

Toward the end of the month, beaver can be seen coming on land once again as their winter food supply begins to dwindle. The wide, upsloping path they leave never fails to catch the eye. It looks almost as if a sled has been pulled over the snow. This is often an item of interest and wonder to the groups I am leading on late February nature hikes at the Adirondack Park VIC at Newcomb.

Toward the end of the month, the pungent aroma of the striped skunk starts to permeate the night air. This pernicious odor is actually a function of the annual mating ritual. When the crows return from the agricultural lands of the St. Lawrence Valley, the stage is set for the eons-old cycle of the land to start anew with the month of March!

Photo by Uta Wister

A peaceful stream in mid-summer

EPILOGUE

2005

As the present year progresses, I have taken to serious musing on things past. This process has been facilitated by the meticulous nature notes and journal I have kept over the past three decades. An analysis of the changes that have crept in over the years has been simply amazing.

It is a truism that nothing in nature is static. Impending global climate change appears to be giving a big boost to nature's dynamism.

Climate change indeed seems to be indicated in the emergence of bird song in the spring, which appears to be commencing earlier and earlier each year. My records, kept over the years, reveal that the chances of hearing singing male birds has gotten earlier as the years have rolled by. This year, 2005, was the earliest ever, with a detectable background of song already in place by the end of April.

Another sign that could indicate the effects of global warming is the arrival of the horrors foisted upon humans by biting insects coming upon the stage much sooner each spring. Traditionally, I recall black flies as not being much of a problem until well into the third week of May. Their presence is generally now felt before the first week in May has elapsed. Mosquitoes, too, seem to be arriving on the scene much earlier; these pests now present an obstacle to the enjoyment of late May evenings. Black flies, however, do appear to be less of an annoyance the past few years, and I attribute this to an anthropological factor: the application of the bacteriological control agent, Bti — or *Bacillus thuringiensis israelensis*, for you biologists out there — in the running brooks where black-fly larvae hatch. The annoyances caused by mosquitoes, meanwhile, continue in an unabated fashion, as does the plague of diurnal deer flies and nocturnal punkies, which generally wait until June to torment local residents and visitors. If anything, the pestilence caused by these winged horrors seems to be getting more severe. The present year either reflects this situation or the fact that my tolerance for them has decreased.

Other changes in wildlife numbers or timing are due to normal ecological processes or to more or less regular fluctuations on cycles in the population. The prodigious outbreak of population in both the Eastern and forest tent caterpillars are almost certainly in the latter category. After a virtual absence of well over a decade, they appeared for the second straight year in 2005 and proceeded to consume wide swaths of St. Lawrence County's arboreal vegetation. The Eastern tent caterpillars completely stripped the leaves of large black cherry trees this year; in past years, they were content to merely defoliate a few small branches or so. The forest tent caterpillar — which, in the non-outbreak years, was not even in evidence — was considerably more catholic in taste, defoliating whole groves of aspen, white ash and sugar maple, among others. Although apparently a regular, cyclical occurrence, the sight of these hardwoods totally without leaves in mid-June was still a difficult sight to endure. As the caterpillars left the trees, to either crawl into cocoons or seek other trees to feed upon, they left a brownish stain blanketing the highways, a stain that appeared at first to be a massive oil slick. I actually had to alight from my vehicle to ascertain what it was.

Nature, however, provides a silver lining for every cloud: This caterpillar eruption has provided food for the first cuckoos I have encountered in a decade. Over the past two years, I have observed both species of cuckoos in a number of locations, waxing merrily and being quite vocal about the bounteous supply of protein that a provident nature has supplied to them.

Cyclical processes also probably account for the large numbers of hares appearing roadside in 2005. Snowshoe hares are famous for extreme cycles in the far north, but in the Adirondacks, these cycles are modified; their predators have greater diversity in their food supply here. Still, the cycle does exist in the North Country to a lesser degree; and when hares are near the top of the local cycle, they will be seen in greater numbers. 2005 is apparently one of these years.

The red foxes, mainly pups, that are proliferating along highways in the summer of 2005 are probably a function of normal, though irregular, ecological processes. The advent of the Eastern coyote in the Great South Woods has restricted red foxes mainly to roadsides and the vicinity of human habitation. The coyotes exclude the foxes from extensive areas of the forest, both by out-competing them for prey and by preying directly upon the foxes. The abundance of insects at three roadside locales in summer also serves to entice foxes to their vicinity. The lack of wariness among the young foxes often leads to their demise. On an evening trip from Lake Clear to Star Lake, I sighted eight red foxes at three different locations; three of these animals were pups who had been hit by vehicles at two locations.

Other changes to which I am attuned this summer have arisen strictly from anthropological sources. Foremost here is the decline in activities traditionally associated with the natural landscape. Berries, bullheads, and bullfrogs still abound; what does not is the will and desire to harvest them as of old. I recall vividly the image of people of varying ages and backgrounds proliferating across the area's wildland carrying buckets to harvest the berry crop. Starting with blueberries, progressing to red raspberries and blackberries, all were collected as they came into fruit. The numbers partaking of this pleasant pastime have dwindled sharply, so that nowadays it is confined mostly to the elderly.

I also can recall another relic of the past: the shimmering glare of a thousand sparks of light illuminating the nocturnal blackness as hordes of bullhead fishermen partook of the favorite pastime along the shores of local water bodies. Alas, that is no more; the same is the case with local people procuring their own frog legs to dine upon. So avid were these froggers in years past that they kept their favorite ponds as much a secret as brook trout fishermen kept their favorite fishing hole. Why these avocations have now become so scarce remains somewhat of a mystery to me. Perhaps it is both the result of a culture of plenty that currently exists as well as myriad new distractions that have recently arrived to compete with the more mundane woodland hobbies of yore.

The last topic to discuss is the question of actual wildlife sightings. This subject is quite complex, as many variable factors enter into the equation of what wildlife is seen. This topic is important to many people who reside in or visit the Adirondacks, as they usually have a keen interest in viewing wildlife — particularly some of the rare and more charismatic examples that are restricted to our regions. A thought to keep always in mind is that sightings of many of these uncommon and elusive species in this heavily forested area are very problematic. Any such glimpses are to be cherished, and thanks ought to be given for them to the Creator — at least, this is what I strongly feel. I have seen four bobcats in the wild during my more than three decades of tramping the Great South Woods. Renowned and legendary woodsman, Clarence

Petty, has seen "only eight or so" in his intimate love affair of more than nine decades with the Adirondack forest.

As discouraging as these figures might appear, the odds on the chances for a positive sighting can be significantly increased under certain circumstances. One of these is to have the key to barred gates and have the freedom to continually traverse the many back-country private roads of the Great South Woods. Two friends who have access to such roads — one at a Scout camp, the other at Camp Sagamore — have each informed me that they have also seen eight bobcats in little more than a decade.

High numbers of ruffed grouse and meadow voles, both cyclical, will also lead to a greater chance of seeing both bobcats and fishers. In fact, although I have seen numerous fishers over the year, several years usually go by without a single sighting. Sightings then begin to proliferate, probably at the peak of the prey cycle.

This year, I am seeing short-tailed shrews everywhere; but since many mammalian predators seem to be repelled by their toxicity, I do not feel they lead to an upsurge in predator sightings. The increase in meadow voles will also lead to more frequent sightings of both species of weasel. This is confirmed by the fact that I usually see these two small mustelids only when the vole population is at its four-year peak.

Overall wildlife sightings have generally increased during my period of living in the Great South Woods. I attribute this mainly to a decline in hunting in the region. Hunting license sales have been declining, year by year, for the past two decades or so. Like the decline in traditional wildlife pursuits mentioned earlier, this decline in hunting is probably the direct result of the numerous competing options now available to the younger generation.

Although definitely auguring well for wildlife in the long run, I must admit to mixed emotions about the decline of these traditional woodland pursuits. All of them, including responsible legal hunting, have been so much a part of the life of our wildlands that they almost appear to be permanent. My cup of nostalgia is overflowing as I dwell upon them, and I fervently hope they will be revived by a future generation.

Photo courtesy Natural History Museum of the Adirondacks

The author making his point during a nature walk.